Healing with Astrology

Sue Lilly

www.capallbann.co.uk

Healing With Astrology

©2002 Sue Lilly

ISBN 186163 184 7

ALL RIGHTS RESERVED

No part of this publication may be reproduced, stored in a retrieval system or transmitted in any form or by any means, electronic, mechanical, photocopying, scanning, recording or otherwise without the prior written permission of the author and the publisher.

Cover design by Paul Mason

Published by:

Capall Bann Publishing
Freshfields
Chieveley
Berks
RG20 8TF

Contents

Introduction — 1

Chapter 1 Signs of the Zodiac and their Elements — 4

Chapter 2 Where the Astrological Information is Stored — 12

Chapter 3 Assessment Technique No.1 — 26

Chapter 4 The Biochemic Tissue Salts — 32

Chapter 5 Using Bach Flower Remedies — 36

Chapter 6 Taking a Deeper Look at the Elements and Mode Assessment — 44

Chapter 7 The Planets — 50

Chapter 8 Planets in Relationship to Each Other — 61

Chapter 9 Healing Strategies using Astrology — 73

Chapter 10 Example of an Astrology Healing Assessment — 81

Chapter 11 Further Explorations with Transits — 94

Chapter 12 Further Exploration for the Spiritual Path — 108

About the author:

Sue Lilly has been working as a professional astrologer for over twenty years. She served as Chairman and Astrological Administrator for the British Astrological and Psychic Society (BAPS) during which time she wrote a certificate course on natal astrology for the Society. She also spent a year as Chairman of the Advisory Panel for Astrological Education. Sue specialises in teaching in a way that takes some of the mystery out of many topcs and with astrology especially, allowing it to be easily accessible to anyone.

Healing with Astrology

Introduction

Astrology holds a fascination for many people, even if that interest is limited to looking up sun-sign information or daily 'stars' in a newspaper. No matter how much the scientific and learned members of our society point out the absurdity of the practice, there is something intangible and compelling about looking at astrology columns in the press. In the last ten years with phone lines having been set up for astrology readings and information, who really knows how many people dip into astrology on a day to day basis?

From its early days until about three hundred years ago, people who were astrologers, were also astronomers, philosophers, scientists and healers. As thinking became more 'head' orientated towards science and logic, astrology and astronomy parted company, and the skills of the healer/astrologer began to be lost. Herbalists, following the guidance of Culpepper, continued to use cycles of nature to help them, but in general, astrology started to tumble into disrepute.

Records and rumours suggest that astrologers were consulted during various wars, such as World War II, when planning campaigns, and that world leaders sometimes check the astrology before taking decisions. For the public, the astrology columns in the press are all that remain.

When I began studying astrology in the 1970's I was already interested in healing. I found to my surprise that very few astrologers seemed to be plugged in to where I was and it was not easy indulging my interest in astrology, healing and the path of the Soul. In the 1970's and early 80's, to draw up a chart you needed to be a mathematician and work logarithms as well working out what the chart meant at the end of it. By the time I was teaching astrology in the mid 80's calculators and computer programmes were starting to emerge. This had the wonderful effect of opening out astrology to a huge number of people who would have otherwise steered clear because of the calculations. In effect, those developments enabled astrology to emerge from its elitist position.

Several years ago I lectured on healing and astrology at the Astrological Association's annual conference. Having developed a sneaky way of combining kinesiology and astrology to give a very powerful but simple healing tool, I was keen to get fellow astrologers interested. I guess, for the first time, it really sank in that many astrologers were not interested in applying their skills for use in holistic healing. The emphasis was then and continues to be on the psychological applications of astrological information.

Healers, on the other hand, now have access to astrological charts through the myriads of computer programmes and charts services available and I found they were interested in using astrological data to augment their skills and knowledge. From that I concluded that teaching healers to use astrology was likely to be more use to the population than teaching astrologers about healing.

This book is intended to act as a guide for a complete beginner, in both astrology and healing, and to act as food for thought for a more seasoned practitioner in both. The information sheets in the Appendices can be freely copied so that they can be used alongside this book.

Many thanks go to Colin Miles of Astrocalc for permission to duplicate astrology charts generated by the Astrocalc computer programme. (Contact address at the back of the book). Thanks, also, to 'Robert' and his family for permission to use his case history as an example. A final special vote of thanks to my husband Simon for reading, correcting and making suggestions to help a non-astrologer to understand the text.

Sue Lilly
Exminster, August 2001

Chapter 1

Signs of the Zodiac and their Elements

The term 'zodiac', meaning 'circle of animals' or 'celestial way', was coined by the Babylonians, who were the first to have totem animals representing twelve divisions of the year. Babylonian Clay tablets held in numerous museums confirm this, with some dating from 722-705BC.

The signs of the zodiac have been linked to parts of the body since the times of the Greek, Hipparchus of Nicacea, (161-127BC). Although Hippocrates (460-377BC), also from Greece, is often accepted as working out the relationship between the stars and the human body, it was indeed Aristotle (384-322BC), yet another Greek, who gave the broad basis of astrology and healing we know today.

The description of these sign correspondences are still widely used.

Aries - head

Taurus - thyroid, pituitary, neck, throat.

Gemini - respiratory system, upper back

Cancer - digestive system, mid back

Leo - cardiac & circulatory system

Virgo - solar plexus, pyloric valve, pancreas, liver, lumbar

Libra - kidneys, urinary bladder, sacrum

Scorpio - bladder, adrenals, ovaries, testes, large intestine, coccyx

Sagittarius - musculature, thighs, hips

Capricorn - skin, knees

Aquarius - circulation, shins, ankles

Pisces - feet, tendons

Several authors have added to this list, but in essence it remains one of the best and simplest of guides - the signs in order, moving from the head, downwards to the feet.

Figure 1 - Signs of The Zodiac and Parts of the Body

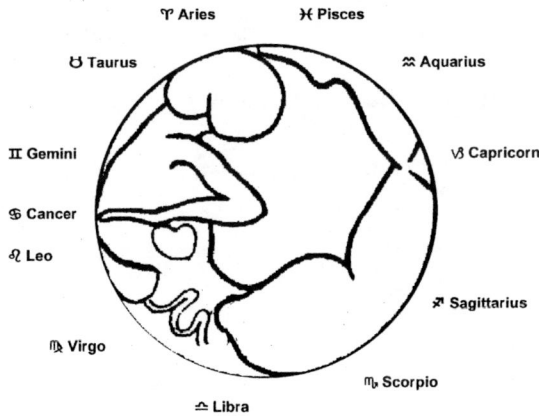

In healing and astrology the signs of the zodiac have two roles. The first role, courtesy of Hipparchus, gives an idea WHERE in the body the energy of the signs tends to work.

The second role of the signs, as in most other types of astrology, is to describe HOW certain energies are liable to work. Here each sign is given a short set of keywords to describe the sort of energy:

Aries - immediate, creative, original, survival, energetic, direct, fast

Taurus - practical, reliable, possessive, sensitive, fertile, steady

Gemini - restless, changeable, inventive, adaptable, intelligent, superficial

Cancer - protective, trusty, nurturing, needs security, caring, remembers

Leo - warm, organising, affectionate, confident, proud, obvious

Virgo - serving, clear, precise, nervous, skilful, practical

Libra - sociable, uniting, balancing, seeks peace, artistic

Scorpio- deep, secretive, passionate, stubborn, intense, healing

Sagittarius - expansive, generous, loud, exaggerates, insatiable, optimistic

Capricorn - disciplined, loyal, ambitious, organising, shy, humourous

Aquarius - fair, eccentric, loyal, aloof, restless, independent, idealistic

Pisces - imaginative, vague, sensitive, unseen, creative

In this book we will make use of both ways of using the signs of the zodiac. There is a table at the back of the book (Appendix 3) that you can copy so that you can have the keywords to hand when you work with astrological information.

Elements

Another Greek philosopher and doctor Empedocles, (490-430BC), saw each of the signs of the zodiac having an element associated with it, one of four - Fire, Earth, Air and Water. He stated that these four elements were seen to be the source of 'love and hate and above all, diseases'.

Each element has three signs ascribed to it. The traits common to the three signs can be found in the description of the element.

Where one element is predominant a person, they exhibit particular characteristics in their behaviour and outlook. The positive and negative traits are both often evident, side by side. Disruption or disease within an individual, often brings about an increase in the negative traits. Medical diagnosis several hundred years ago took notice of these changes. Nowadays, possibly only a homeopath, herbalist or complementary therapist is likely to take this type of approach.

Elements give a general description of how signs work

Fire Element
The element of Fire is linked to the signs of Aries, Leo and Sagittarius, and describes what was known as the *choleric* temperament.

Fire Element characteristics:
Touchy
Strong emotions, short lasting
Bitter and wounded
Irascible
Self confident
No time for details
Overbearing, ambitious, decisive
Loyal, proud
Arrogant, bad temper
Reckless
Strong
Active
Idealistic
Courageous
Helpful, kind
Imposes own authority
Fanatic
Self-indulgent

The element of Earth is linked to the signs of Taurus, Virgo and Capricorn (called the *phlegmatic* temperament)

Earth Element characteristics
Fussy
Obstinate
Traditional
Conservative
Practical
Reliable
Lazy
Provides necessities

Deep understanding
Refines
Hoards resources

The element of Air (the *sanguine* temperament) is linked to the signs of Gemini, Libra and Aquarius.

Air Element characteristics
Excitable
Interested
Short attention span
Unreliable
Impulsive
Optimistic
Co-operative
Inventive
Objective
Superficial
Aloof

The element of Water (*melancholic temperament*) is linked to the signs of Cancer, Scorpio and Pisces.

Water Element characteristics
Cautious
Deep
Mistrustful
Worry of the future
Jealous
Industrious
Solitary
Love of nature
Ungrounded
Fantasises
Exaggerates
Sensitive
Artistic

Romantic
Reserved

Modes of Action

The signs of the zodiac were also divided in a different way, into three groups, corresponding with the seasons of the year. Each group has four signs. The phrases describe the common characteristics that the group of signs share. They are all associated with how the signs work.

Cardinal Signs are related to the beginning of each season. (Aries, Cancer, Libra and Capricorn)

Sensitive to the environment
Easily influence
Hard to say no
Learn to take care of self
Object of projection
Mirror for others
Need to learn discrimination
Enterprising
Impatient
Controlling
Forceful

Fixed signs are related to seasons when they are established. (Taurus, Leo, Scorpio, Aquarius)

Determined
Single minded
Need to become more open and adaptable
Consistent
Traditional
A lot in reserve
Formal
Resists change

Mutable signs are related to seasons when they are changing.(Gemini, Virgo, Sagittarius, Pisces)

Adaptable
Martyr
Need to become more focused on self
Excessive mental activity
Exaggerates
Sees details, not the whole
Gives up easily
Makes the most out of any situation

When you know the element and mode of any sign, by combining the two sets of keywords, you can outline the way the sign works.

For example, Aries is a fire sign in the cardinal mode (active and enterprising), Leo is a fire sign in the fixed mode (active and determined) and Sagittarius is a fire sign in the mutable mode (active and adaptable).

Chapter 2

Where the Astrological Information is Stored

The information that you need to use to assess healing for an individual with astrology can be found in two main places. The best type of information is to have access to a copy of the individual's natal or birth chart. For an accurate natal chart, a person would need to supply the date, time and place of their birth. If someone does not know the time of birth, a chart drawn up for dawn or noon can be used. If you don't have a birth chart you can access a significant amount of information from an ephemeris or set of planetary tables. This is ideal if someone only knows their birth date.

Collecting the data from a natal astrological chart

The amount of information on the chart sheet itself will depend to some extent on the source and type of chart. All the information you need will, however, be on the chart-disc itself.

The astrological chart

The astrological chart is essentially a snapshot, from the Earth's point of view, of the planets, sun and moon as they appear against the backdrop of the stars. In most natal astrology carried out in the West, this is applied using what is called the Tropical Zodiac [1]. The signs of the zodiac, planets, Sun and Moon are all shown by a type of astrological shorthand.

Figure 2 - An Example Chart

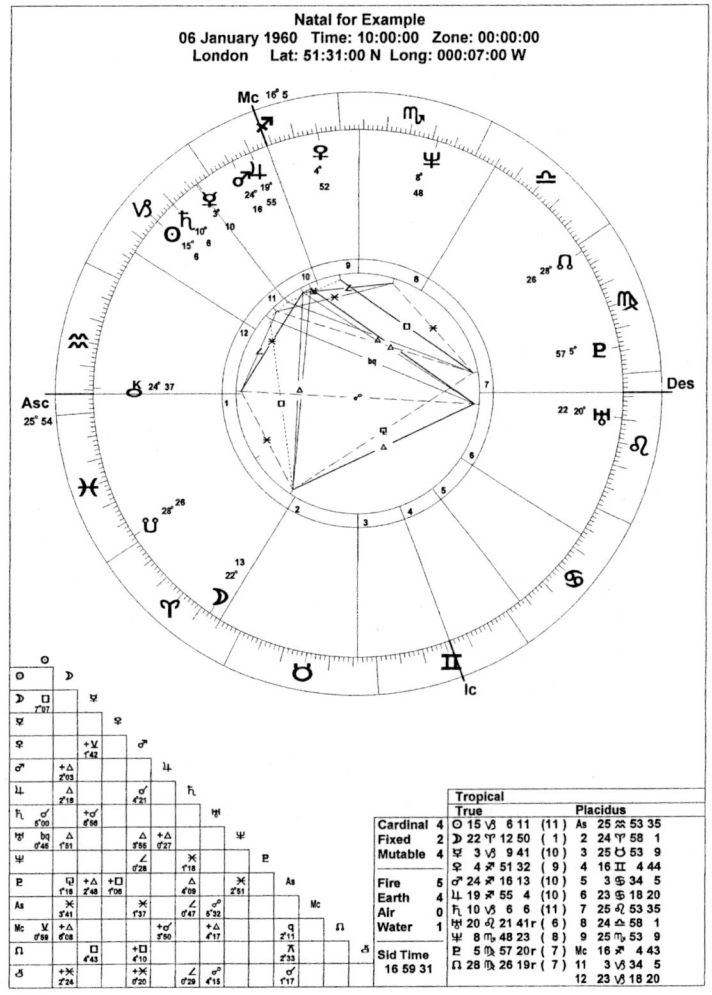

The outermost circle contains the glyphs of the signs of the zodiac, listed in an anticlockwise direction. They are:-

♈   Aries

♉   Taurus

♊   Gemini

♋   Cancer

♌   Leo

♍   Virgo

♎   Libra

♏   Scorpio

♐   Sagittarius

♑   Capricorn

♒   Aquarius

♓   Pisces

The actual style of the glyphs may vary depending on the source and the typeface used. If the Virgo and Scorpio glyphs are very similar, you can always look to the signs either side to confirm which of the two you are looking at as the signs always come in the same order.

The next circle inwards shows another set of glyphs - the shorthand for the planets, Sun and Moon. There may also be other glyphs present. All are shown in the sign that acts as the backdrop to the planet, when it is viewed from the Earth.

Figure 3 - the Zodiac Circle

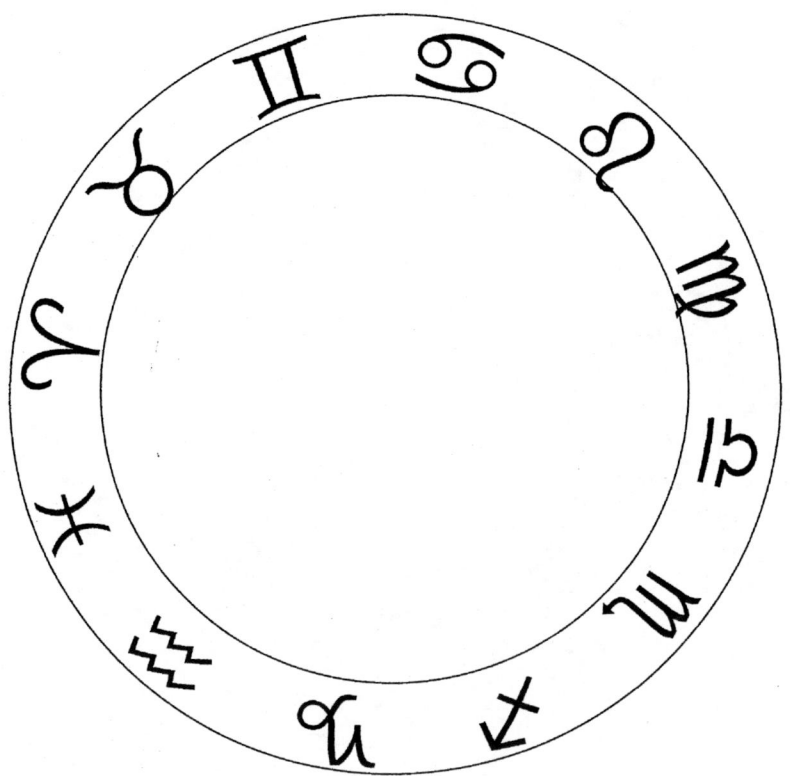

Figure 4 - The Zodiac Circle with Planetary Glyphs

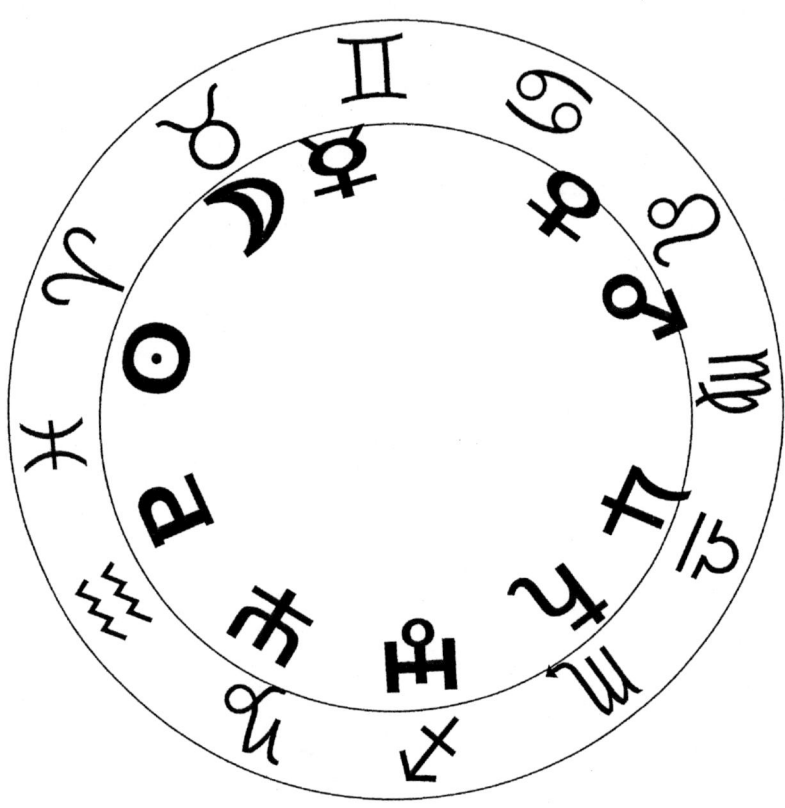

16

For example: When we say someone is sun-sign Pisces, this means that they were born when the sun appeared against the backdrop of Pisces, as viewed from the Earth. The glyph for the sun (top), will appear in the section of the chart bordered by Pisces.

Figure 5 - Planets in Signs

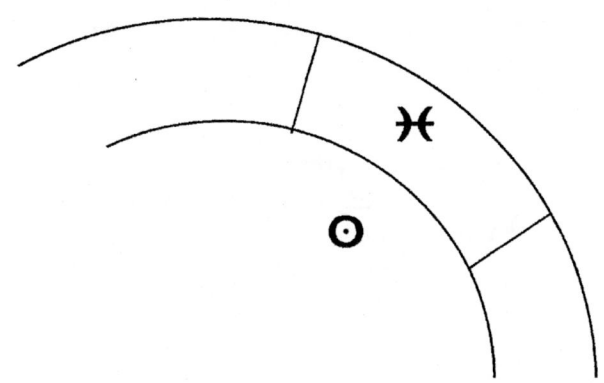

The glyphs of the planets, Sun and Moon are:

☉	Sun
☽	Moon
☿	Mercury
♀	Venus
♂	Mars
♃	Jupiter
♄	Saturn

⛢   Uranus

♆   Neptune

♇ or ⚳   Pluto

⚷   Chiron

As with the glyphs of the signs, these too may vary slightly in design.

The central area of the natal chart is taken up with lines of various colours and/or qualities. These are shorthand for the mathematical relationship (angles) and resonance between each planet, sun and moon. These types of relationships are called 'aspects'. We will deal with some of these later in the book.

Other Significant Points

Other glyphs that may be present that can have important use in the assessment process.

☊   **North Node**

☋   **South Node**

These represent the point in the zodiac where the apparent path of the Sun cuts across the path of the Moon. They always register in signs that are opposite to one another. Some types of chart will only indicate the North Node, leaving you to note down where the South Node occurs.

Known Time of Birth

If the chart is reasonably accurate, then the Nodes of the Moon, Ascendant and Midheaven can also be included.

The Ascendant (**As**) or (Asc) is the left half of the line across the middle of the whole chart that represents the actual horizon at the time of birth. Sometimes this line cuts the chart completely in two, though more usually, the middle section is omitted because it crowds the centre area too much. Quite often it has the abbreviation '**As**' or 'Asc' where it cuts the left side of the chart.

Figure 6 - Ascendant

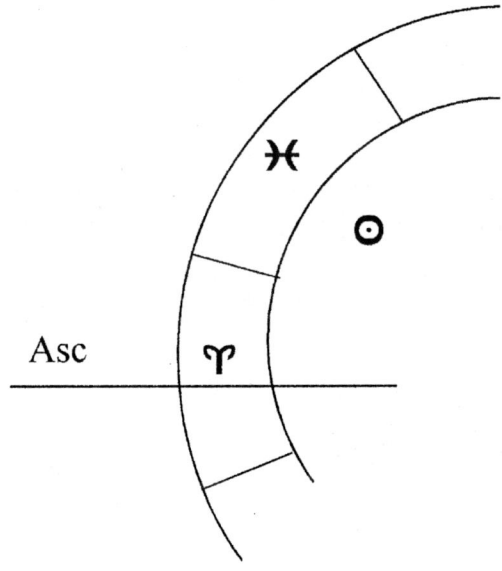

The sign of the Ascendant is the zodiac sign the 'Asc' passes through. In an accurate chart, the Ascendant represents the lens through which the person appears to the world and through which they express themselves by their mannerisms and behaviour. There is also evidence that this sign can indicate certain types of physical attributes (body-type, height etc).

The Midheaven (**Mc**) or Medium Coeli can also be used in an assessment. This is the point on the natal chart where the sun would reach its highest point on that day. It is shown on the chart by a vertical, or near vertical line that cuts the chart in two. The **Mc** is the place where the line cuts the zodiac circle in the upper half of the chart. It is indicative of the most public mask of an individual, often linked to ego.

Figure 7 - Midheaven

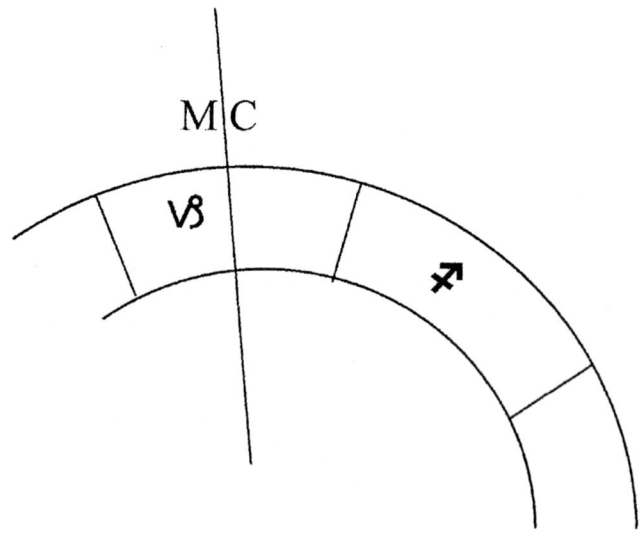

Unknown Time of Birth

When the time of an individual's birth is unknown, it is unwise to include the '**As**' and '**Mc**' in the assessment, as charts drawn up in these circumstances are often drawn up for noon or dawn. These charts can still be used, but as well as ignoring the '**As**' and '**Mc**', care needs to be taken over the sign of the Moon.

The Moon moves through a zodiac sign every two and a half days. Often, within the space of 24 hours, the Moon will move from one sign to another. Any chart where the birth time is unknown needs to be studied closely for how close the Moon is the beginning or end of a sign. [Each zodiac sign takes up 30 degrees, one twelfth of the circle of the chart]

The Moon, moves one degree in about 2 hours. If a chart is drawn up for noon or dawn and you know the person was born in late evening, for example, you can estimate where the Moon is liable to be. This could show whether it has changed signs.

Similarly, if you have a general chart drawn at noon and the person was born in the early morning, estimation of the Moon's place might take it into the previous sign.

Reading from Planetary Tables

If you don't have access to somebody's chart, you can read the most important information you need straight from the planetary tables or ephemeris. These tables can be found in small, yearly booklets or in larger books covering 50 or 100-years. They can come as 'Midnight' tables, that is, all the data is geared to midnight (00.00hrs), or as 'Noon' where all the data is geared to placements at noon or 12.00hrs. For the purpose of this work it matters little which type you have access to.

Ephemeris October 1952 (Noon)

Ephemeris October 1952 (Noon)

Day	Sid.T	Sun	Moon	N Node	Merc	Venus	Mars	Jup.	Saturn	Uranus	Nept.	Pluto
1	12:40:39	8Li14	10Pi32	18Aq55	13Li35	4Sc37	22Sg30	20Ta2R	16Li45	18Cn18	20Li57	22Le35
2	12:44:35	9 13	25 21	18 52	15 17	5 51	23 11	20 8	16 52	18 19	20 59	22 37
3	12:48:32	10 12	10Ar4	18 49	16 57	7 5	23 53	20 3	16 59	18 20	21 1	22 38
4	12:52:29	11 11	24 35	18 46	18 37	8 18	24 35	19 59	17 7	18 21	21 4	22 39
5	12:56:25	12 10	8Ta46	18 43	20 17	9 32	25 16	19 54	17 14	18 22	21 6	22 41
6	13:0:22	13 10	22 34	18 39	21 55	10 46	25 58	19 49	17 21	18 23	21 8	22 42
7	13:4:19	14 9	5Ge56	18 36	23 33	11 59	26 40	19 43	17 29	18 24	21 10	22 43
8	13:8:15	15 8	18 52	18 33	25 10	13 13	27 23	19 38	17 36	18 25	21 13	22 45
9	13:12:11	16 7	1Cn25	18 30	26 46	14 26	28 5	19 33	17 43	18 26	21 15	22 46
10	13:16:8	17 7	13 38	18 27	28 21	15 40	28 47	19 27	17 51	18 27	21 17	22 47
11	13:20:4	18 6	25 38	18 23	29 56	16 53	29 30	19 21	17 58	18 27	21 19	22 48
12	13:24:1	19 5	7Le28	18 20	1Sc30	18 7	0Cp13	19 15	18 5	18 28	21 21	22 50
13	13:27:57	20 5	19 15	18 17	3 3	19 20	0 55	19 9	18 13	18 29	21 24	22 51
14	13:31:54	21 4	1Vi4	18 14	4 35	20 34	1 38	19 3	18 20	18 29	21 26	22 52
15	13:35:51	22 4	12 58	18 11	6 7	21 47	2 21	18 56	18 27	18 30	21 28	22 53
16	1£:39:47	23 3	25 3	18 8	7 39	23 1	3 4	18 50	18 35	18 30	21 30	22 54
17	13:43:44	24 3	7Li19	18 4	9 9	24 14	3 47	18 43	18 42	18 31	21 33	22 55
18	13:47:40	25 2	19 50	18 1	10 39	25 28	4 31	18 36	18 49	18 31	21 35	22 56
19	13:51:37	26 2	2Sc35	17 58	12 8	26 41	5 14	18 29	18 57	18 31	21 37	22 57
20	13:55:33	27 2	15 34	17 55	13 37	27 55	5 57	18 22	19 4	18 32	21 39	22 58
21	13:59:30	28 2	28 47	17 52	15 5	29 8	6 41	18 15	19 11	18 32	21 42	22 59
22	14:3:27	29 1	12Sg10	17 49	16 32	0Sg21	7 24	18 8	19 19	18 32	21 44	23 0
23	14:7:23	0Sc 1	25 44	17 45	17 59	1 35	8 8	18 0	19 26	18 32	21 46	23 1
24	14:11:20	1 1	9Cp28	17 42	19 25	2 48	8 52	17 53	19 33	18 32	21 48	23 2
25	14.15:16	2 1	23 19	17 39	20 50	4 1	9 36	17 45	19 40	18 32R	21 50	23 3
26	14:19:13	3 1	7Aq20	17 36	22 14	5 15	10 20	17 38	19 48	18 32	21 53	23 4
27	14:23:9	4 0	21 28	17 33	23 38	6 28	11 4	17 30	19 55	18 32	21 55	23 5
28	14:27:6	5 0	5Pi44	17 29	25 0	7 41	11 48	17 22	20 2	18 32	21 57	23 5
29	14:31:2	6 0	20 4	17 26	26 2	8 54	12 32	17 14	20 9	18 31	21 59	23 6
30	14:34:59	7 0	4Ar27	17 23	27 43	10 8	13 16	17 6	20 16	18 31	22 1	23 7
31	14:38:56	8 0	18 46	17 20	29 2	11 21	14 0	16 59	20 23	18 31	22 4	23 8

If you are going to use them as a basis for calculation though, you need to remember which sort you have, because if affects the maths!

Although ephemerides vary a little, their basic design is the same. There are sections for each month of a year, with a series of columns, showing zodiac placement.

For the purposes of this book, the first column, headed 'Sid.T' can be ignored. This gives the Sidereal Time[2] or Star (astronomical) Time at noon for each day of the month. We can also ignore the 'R' in the column headed 'Jup.', and where the 'R' also appears on the 25th October for Uranus. 'R' refers to 'retrograde' planetary motion 3 and can occur in any planet column, apart from the Sun and Moon. The column headed 'N.Node', does not have an 'R' in this ephemeris, but all of the Moon's Node placements are always retrograde. The assessments in this book do not require knowledge of retrograde planetary movement.

Each of the planets then has a column, showing the number of degrees of the sign they appear at for a given date.

Notice, for this example month, on the 'Sun' column, the column starts off as Libra and then on the 23rd of the month, changes to Scorpio. Similarly, the column belonging to the Moon, the sign changes every 2-3 days.

This particular ephemeris shows the signs by abbreviation of their names. Some ephemeris tables, give the signs by their glyph.

This ephemeris does not give a placement for Chiron, some do. If you come across an ephemeris without Chiron, if you have no other way of finding out where Chiron is (from another ephemeris, natal chart etc), it is best to leave Chiron out of the assessment.

Chiron, a planetoid, was discovered in 1977 orbiting between Saturn and Uranus. There has been a lot of research and speculation about the energy that Chiron represents. It is included here, because it seems to have relevance to health.

Footnotes

1 - Tropical Zodiac

The Tropical Zodiac is the name given to the sequence of the signs of the zodiac that begin with 0 degrees Aries, at the Spring Equinox, around the 20th March each year. Most Western astrology uses the Tropical Zodiac.

The other type of zodiac, the Sidereal Zodiac, is used by astronomers and some astrologers. The astrological sign of the Spring Equinox is taken from distant stars. Due to the way the Earth's axis wobbles in space, the Spring Equinox point moves very slowly backwards through the signs of the zodiac. It takes over 25,000 years to move through all the signs. The Spring Equinox in the Sidereal Zodiac, presently occurs at 5 degrees Pisces. The last time the Tropical and Sidereal zodiacs coincided was 221AD.

2 - Sidereal Time

Sidereal Time or Star Time, is time as gauged by the rotation of the Earth and not by a clock. The Earth takes 23 hours 56 minutes and 4 seconds to rotate, so with the passing of each day, clock time and sidereal time differ. This difference is approximately 10 seconds per hour. The Sidereal Time given in a noon ephemeris is the Sidereal Time equivalent to noon on that day. With a midnight ephemeris, the Sidereal Time is given equivalent to midnight on the day in question.

3 - Retrograde Motion

Retrograde motion or 'moving backwards' occurs as an optical illusion caused by viewing planets against distant stars when seen from the Earth. The illusion occurs because the Earth itself is also moving around the Sun. These backwards movements are shown in the ephemeris or on a chart by 'R' after the glyph or position of a planet.

Chapter 3

Assessment Technique No.1

Self-help techniques associated with astrology that are easy to use are often centred around the sun-sign of an individual. This, at best, is only a small part of the jigsaw of energies that make up a person, and can be very misleading. Using basic astrological data from a natal chart or read straight from the ephemeris (planetary tables) for someone's birth day, a broader and more complete picture emerges. This straightforward technique only needs the information of the signs for each planet in an individual's astrological data. If you have access to an accurate natal chart, you can also include the Ascendant and Midheaven and Nodes of the moon.

Begin by listing the planets, and other points of the chart, down one side of a sheet of blank paper or copy Worksheet 1 at the back of this book.

1. When you have the planets listed, look through the birth data and list the sign that each planet or point occurs in.

2. Look up the Element and Mode of Action for that sign, and list or enter it onto the worksheet.

As an example, we will work from the birth date of Sophie.

Sophie was born on the 26th October 1952, at 6am, local time, in London. With this information we can work from a chart (as we have been given all the data, see Figure 9) or from the ephemeris. (Ephemeris extract is on page 22, Figure 8)

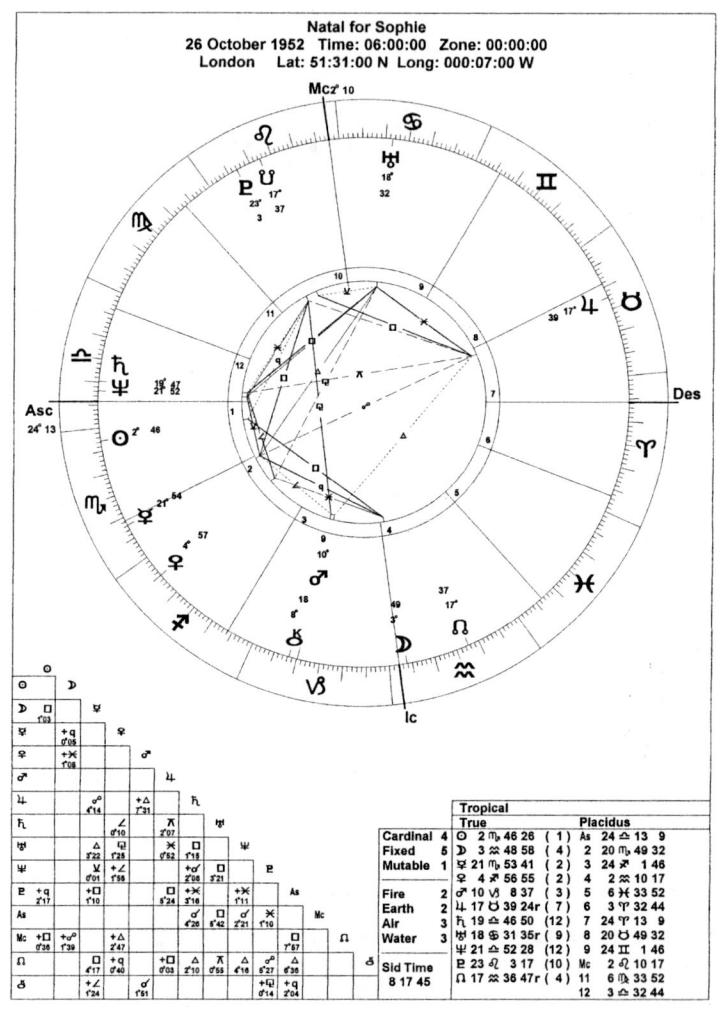

Figure 9 - Sophie's Natal Chart

Worksheet 1 for Sophie

Planet	Planet	Sign	Sign	Element	Mode of Action
☉	Sun	♏	Scorpio	Water	Fixed
☽	Moon	♒	Aquarius	Air	Fixed
☿	Mercury	♏	Scorpio	Water	Fixed
♀	Venus	♐	Sagittarius	Fire	Mutable
♂	Mars	♑	Capricorn	Earth	Cardinal
♃	Jupiter	♉	Taurus	Earth	Fixed
♄	Saturn	♎	Libra	Air	Cardinal
♅	Uranus	♋	Cancer	Water	Cardinal
♆	Neptune	♎	Libra	Air	Cardinal
♇	Pluto	♌	Leo	Fire	Fixed
⚷	Chiron	♑	Capricorn	Earth	Cardinal
As	Ascendant	♎	Libra	Air	Cardinal
Mc	Midheaven	♌	Leo	Fire	Fixed
☊	North Node	♒	Aquarius	Air	Fixed
☋	South Node	♌	Leo	Fire	Fixed

Figure 10 - Worksheet 1

3. When you have completed your data collection simply count how many times each of the elements occur, and then how many times each 'mode of action' occurs. Enter your findings into the table:

Totals for Sophie:

Element	Element Totals	Mode	Mode Totals
Fire	4	Cardinal	6
Earth	3	Fixed	8
Air	5	Mutable	1
Water	3		

Figure 11 - Element and Mode Totals for Sophie

The totals in the elements will show you which of the elements are dominant and which are lacking.

For Sophie - Air is dominant with a total of over '4' and Earth/Water are lacking, both totalling below '4'.

The totals of the modes will do the same.

For Sophie - Fixed is dominant, totalling more than '5' and Mutable is lacking, totalling considerably less than '5'.

4. We can then re-translate the elements and modes back into their respective signs.

For Sophie   - Air/Fixed is dominant
                  - Earth &Water/Mutable are lacking

These translate back to

        Air/Fixed = Aquarius (Dominant)
        Earth/ Mutable = Virgo (Lacking)
        Water/Mutable = Pisces (Lacking)

This assessment would not be obvious from the chart data on its own. Even in this simplest of forms the information gleaned can be most useful.

Combinations that are dominant indicate energies we use a lot, and are unlikely to absorb or obtain enough from our environment or lifestyle to sustain that use. We can benefit, therefore, from healing modes that link to our dominant energies, as they 'plug the gap'.

Combinations that are lacking indicate energies that our bodies do not recognise or poorly absorb for our well-being. We can benefit from healing modes that correspond to the energies we lack as they underpin and stabilise us.

Having ascertained the signs of the zodiac that are dominant and lacking, the signs can link to correspondences of easily acquired healing tools. In the following chapters, Biochemic Tissue Salts and Bach Flower Remedies are covered, but any system that has astrological links like these can be used (see Appendix 7).

If, when you work these out there is no particular dominance or lack of energy indicated for an individual, you will need to carry out a deeper assessment as outlined later, using Worksheet 2.

Chapter 4

The Biochemic Tissue Salts

Biochemistry describes the chemical changes within all life processes. Different tissues in our bodies are formed by the action of inorganic compounds with organic substances.

The human body is composed of millions of cells, each cell being a perfectly balanced unit. Amongst the constituents of each cell are mineral elements in very small quantities. Since the life of cells is short, new ones are continually being rebuilt. It was recognised over one hundred years ago that if the blood lacked the relevant minerals, the cells created did not function so well.

Dr W Schussler (1828-1898) found that there were 12 mineral salts vital to the well-being of the human body. These are keys to building and repairing our bodies. It is thought that many modern diseases and illnesses can be traced back to lack of subtle layers of nutrition. The mineral salts can also go some way to compensate for depleted soil in which our food is grown or on which it is reared.

Although Dr Schussler's system uses 12 minerals or tissue salts which do appear in the Homeopathic Pharmacopoeia, he states very clearly that the tissue salts are not founded on the 'Law of Similars' or 'Like cures Like' as found in homeopathy. They are used by the body in a direct manner. He goes on to say that each salt could be selected in a homeopathic way as a homeopathic remedy. The tissue salt however, selected on physical symptoms only and is therefore a Biochemic remedy.

The advantage of having minerals in a 6x (6th potency/dilution)^4 is that the body absorbs the energy immediately - the nutrients not needing to go through the digestive process. Although tissue salts are minute amounts, they play a disproportionately large role in routine natural chemical processes.

The astrological links of the tissue salts are well know, and listed in the table below. However, looking at the astrological data obtained from Worksheet 1, a more precise picture emerges, rather than taking just the sun-sign of an individual.

Taking Sophie's birthdata as the example, we can see from her worksheet that although she is a Scorpio sun-sign:

She is dominant in   - Air/Fixed (Aquarius)
She is lacking in   - Earth/Mutable (Virgo)
                              - Water/Mutable (Pisces)

This would translate to her needing
                        Nat Mur (Aquarius)
                        Kali Sulph (Virgo)
                        Ferr Phos (Pisces)

The Biochemic Tissue Salts can be obtained from any good health shop or pharmacy/chemist.

Using Tissue Salts
It is usually recommended by the manufacturers that the tissue salts, which are typically melt-in-the-mouth pilules, be dissolved under the tongue. Since we are dealing in this type of assessment with long term, chronic situations, their guidance is three doses daily.

When working this way, the tissue salt would need to be taken for a month. The situation would then need to be reassessed. It is likely, however, that it would be necessary to return to the salt periodically, as the energy pattern shown by the astrological data is so ingrained. These patterns have been present from birth and would need to be revisited and worked on, from time to time.

Footnotes

4 - potency/dilution
Homeopathic remedies are prepared by diluting one drop of the original product with 10 or 100 drops of water. This mixture is then 'succussed', that is shaken vigorously thousands of times. This is said to potentise the mixture. One drop of this mixture is then diluted in a similar fashion and succused again. This process of dilution and succussion creates homeopathic potencies. The more the substance is diluted and succussed, the higher the potency. Biochemic Tissue Salts are of the 6th (6X) potency, one considered most useful for everyday use. Potencies of 30, 200, 1000 + are often used by homeopaths.

Biochemic Tissue Salts

Sign	Code No	Name	Found In	Can help with
♈	6	Kali Phos	Brain Nerve cells	All temporary 'nervy' conditions, mental stress, sleeplessness, tension
♉	11	Nat Sulph	Intercellular tissue Excess water Liver function	Reduces water retention Liver upsets, detoxifier Hayfever
♊	5	Kali Mur	Saliva Skin cells Fibrin	Swellings, liver problems Constipation, piles Diarrhoea
♋	1	Calc Fluor	Bones, teeth, Walls of blood vessels Connective tissue	Varicose veins, piles Flabbiness Teeth problems
♌	8	Mag Phos	Nerves	Cramps, spasms Colic, headaches
♍	7	Kali Sulph	Skin	Inflammation, catarrh, brittle nails, Palpitations Chills and flushes
♎	10	Nat Phos	Intercellular fluid, Nerves, brain, Bile, acid neutraliser	Rheumatism, gout Gallstones, nausea Loss of appetite
♏	3	Calc Sulph	Connective tissue Blood purifier Liver cells	Acne, skin problems Neuralgia, Pancreas, liver, kidney upsets
♐	12	Silica	Blood, skin, hair Nervous system bones	Cleanser, tonic, joint pain Falling out hair Skin eruptions
♑	2	Calc Phos	Bones, Teeth Gastric juices	Healthy bones, teeth Poor digestion, Chilblains, cramps
♒	9	Nat Mur	Helps with water balance in the body	Circulation, runny colds, Loss of taste, smell All fluid problems 'flu, acne
♓	4	Ferr Phos	Red blood cells	Inflammations Bleeding, Colds

Chapter 5

Using Bach Flower Remedies

Dr Edward Bach (1886 - 1936) was a particularly gifted doctor and researcher. For several years after he qualified as a doctor he investigated the role of specific types of bacteria in the gut that seemed to give a predisposition to types of diseases that were difficult to treat. This first opened his eyes to the personality patterns in the sufferers he saw. He noted that the emotional state of a person was difficult to separate from the disease they were suffering from. Some diseases gave rise to similar emotional patterns in different people. He went on to study homeopathy and create what are known as the 'Bach Bowel Nosodes' of those bacteria. These nosodes he used in such as way that they acted as a type of vaccination for people suffering from a wide range of diseases.

His disillusionment with and movement away from, the conventional treatments of the time centred around the concentration of attention of those treatments on physical health. Like many a gifted healer before him, he knew that to have complete health, the emotions and finer aspects of the person needed to be considered. He eventually gave up his Harley Street practice in order to find remedies that everyone could use from plants and nature.

Inspired by his earlier work on bacteria nosodes he began looking at natural sources, mainly plants, to treat the emotional states he saw as the basis of many diseases. He started to look for plants, herbs and trees that could help with different temperaments.

The first three plants he encountered were Mimulus, Impatiens and Clematis. He created remedies from these in the summer of 1928 in Wales. The remedies were made by what is now known as 'the traditional sunlight method'. That is, the flowers of the plant were floated on spring water in full sunlight. The resulting water was then preserved in brandy.

In 1930 and 1931 he added another nine remedies to these three, to produce what are known as the 'Twelve Healers'. The additional nine were - Gentian, Cerato, Rock Rose, Vervain, Centaury, Scleranthus, Chicory, Agrimony and Water Violet. These were linked to the twelve signs of the zodiac.

In 1933 he made another four, called the 'Four Helpers' - Gorse, Oak, Heather and Rock Water. The Rock Water remedy is simply flowing spring water preserved in brandy. He also created the first combination 'Rescue Remedy' which was a mixture of Clematis, Impatiens and Rock Rose. (He later added Star of Bethlehem and Cherry Plum to create the 'Rescue Remedy' we know today.)

The remaining Three Helpers, Olive, Vine and Wild Oat, (making seven in all), were added in 1934. The Olive and Vine remedies were created by friends in Italy and Switzerland.

He added another nineteen remedies, making a total of thirty eight, in the year before his death. These remedies were made in a different way. The plant material was boiled and the resulting liquid preserved in brandy.

In this book we will only be working with the first nineteen Bach made, as these are the only ones with astrological correspondences. They are also the ones made by what is known as 'the traditional sunlight method'.

The first twelve remedies Dr Bach made, he called the Twelve Healers. In a letter written in October 1933, from Cromer,

Norfolk, he states that he left out the signs and the months in the Twelve Healers as he was still unsure about the exact astrological correspondences. He did acknowledge that the Twelve Healers would assist the understanding of astrology, but he was no expert. He did however enclose a list that was printed in 1933 for those who wished to investigate for themselves.

Interestingly, the 1933 publication goes on to link the personality types with the Moon signs at the time of birth and not the sun-signs as is often supposed in many recent written works.

In the early information on the Bach Remedies, assessment was by the identification of negative emotional states. Although useful, over the years this had led to the plants in the range being closely associated with difficult emotions. It has also led to assessment being used in a very prescriptive manner. So, Pine (Pinus sylvestris), for example, is indicated when people have guilt feelings. The energy of Pine is, of course, much broader in its remit and would be of likely use in many different situations.

More recently writers have included emotions that the person may be striving or working to develop, painting a more complete picture of each remedy. The list included here contains the classical 'key negative emotions' and positive emotions.

Sign	Essence	Key Negative state	Positive state
♈	Impatiens	Impatience, irritable, restless, tense	Energetic, pioneering
♉	Gentian	Over-sensitive, stubborn, single minded, despondent	Practical, nurturing
♊	Cerato	Looks outside for wisdom, too diverse, talkative	Flexible, easy-going
♋	Rock Rose	Over-emotional, attached to past experience and fear	Capable, caring
♌	Vervain	Fixed ideas, demands recognition, wilful	Leadership, warmth
♍	Centaury	Over-anxious to serve others, denying personal path	Thorough, helpful
♎	Scleranthus	Indecision, changing moods, uncertainty	Impartial, creative
♏	Chicory	Obsessive, manipulative, worrier	Resourceful, generous
♐	Agrimony	Ignoring inner pains, superficial moods	Optimistic, outgoing
♑	Mimulus	Materialistic, lack of trust in life, fears	Reliable, works hard
♒	Water Violet	Isolationist, aloof, unapproachable	Independent, unique
♓	Clematis	Escapist, dreamy, vague	Artistic, sensitive

Figure 13 - The Bach Flower Remedies - The Twelve Healers

Originally, there were only four remedies which Dr Bach called the Four Helpers. These were Gorse, Oak, Heather and Rock Water. He realised that these four did not fit the same pattern as the previous twelve. They seemed to indicate another type of state where the person was stuck and where it was difficult to determine which of the Twelve Healers would really be of use.

These first Four Helpers could be successfully linked to the four elements - Fire, Earth, Air and Water.

The First Four Helpers

Element	Essence	Negative State	Positive State
Fire	Gorse	Hopelessness, resignation	Energetic, courageous
Earth	Oak	Stoic, hates failure	Persistent, reliable
Air	Heather	Needs company and to talk, anxious	Communicative, makes connections
Water	Rock Water	Self-denying, hard on themselves	Sensitive, empathic

Figure 14-The Bach Flower Remedies - The First Four Healers

Three more Helpers followed bring the total to seven. These three were Olive, Vine and Wild Oat, and these can be related to the Modes of action

Further Three Helpers

Mode	Bach Essence	Key Negative State	Positive State
Cardinal	Vine	Authoritative, dominant	Wise, confident
Fixed	Olive	Exhausted, weary	Strength, steady
Mutable	Wild Oat	Lack of direction	Adaptable, flexible

Figure 15 - The Bach Flower Remedies - Further Three Helpers

The individual's birth data can thus be used to create a combination of Bach Flower Remedies.

Using Sophie's data as an example, we can see from her chart that she is Moon sign Aquarius, which would indicate the possible use of Water Violet.

From the worksheet we note:

She is dominant in   - Air/Fixed (Aquarius)
She is lacking in   - Earth/ Mutable (Virgo)
                            - Water/Mutable (Pisces)

This would translate to her needing

- Water Violet
- Centaury
- Clematis

However, also having essences that relate to the Element and Modes on their own, we remember that Sophie has:

Fire - 4
Earth - 3
Air - 5
Water - 3

Cardinal - 6
Fixed - 8
Mutable - 1

We could decide that the Elements are fairly balanced. The most obvious quality in the Modes, is Mutable with only a value of 1.

From the Bach Remedy listing, we could suggest that Sophie add Wild Oat (Mutable) to her personal essence combination.

Using the Seven Helpers in this way can be ideal when dealing with someone who has totals for the Elements and/or Modes that are extreme - values of only 1 or 0 for either Elements and Modes or values over 6 for the Elements and over 10 for the Modes. For those people remedies chosen solely from the Seven Helpers can be very useful for in times of crisis.

Using Bach Flower Remedies
Flower and vibrational essences can be used in any number of ways. Traditionally 3 - 7 drops are taken from the bottle and placed under the tongue or in a small glass of water. This process is then repeated 3 or 4 times a day.

Nowadays it is recognised that as a vibrational tool, the essences can be used directly onto the skin, inhaled, sprayed around the body or in some instances, holding a bottle of the essence can have the desired effect. Whichever way you use essences or you suggest other people use essences, remember that if they or you are used to 'taking by mouth' and feel other methods would not work, to stick with the traditional way.

Footnotes

5 - Remedies
Bach Flower Remedies were given their name at a time when there were few, if any, regulations about naming products. Nowadays the word 'remedy' is construed as referring to something that has proven medicinal use. People making flower remedies in a similar way to Dr Bach these days, tend to use other names, such as 'essence' to describe their products.

Unlike homeopathic remedies, the Bach Flower Remedies and other essences are not sequentially diluted and succussed. They are a simple, single dilution of the original preparation.

Chapter 6

Taking a Deeper Look at the Elements and Mode Assessment

With some charts and natal information, Worksheet 1 can fail to give a conclusive assessment. It can be useful, then to take a deeper look at this type of assessment, to highlight deeper patterns at play within an individual.

To do this we use what is known in astrological terms as the 'Rulers' of the signs of the zodiac. These are planets that have a special relationship with specific zodiac signs.

With the discoveries of Uranus, Neptune, Pluto and Chiron this information which goes back to a Babylonian Clay tablet associated with the King Amisadqa, has been augmented.

Worksheet 2 enables you to add the concept of 'Rulers' to your assessment. The 'Ruler' of each sign of the zodiac for each planet from the natal chart is ascertained. That planet's sign, element and mode, as it appears in the individual's chart is then noted.

Figure 16 - Signs and their Ruling Planets

Sign	Symbol	Ancient Ruler	Modern Ruler
Aries	♈	Mars	Mars
Taurus	♉	Venus	Venus
Gemini	♊	Mercury	Mercury
Cancer	♋	Moon	Moon
Leo	♌	Sun	Sun
Virgo	♍	Mercury	Mercury
Libra	♎	Venus	Venus
Scorpio	♏	Mars	Pluto
Sagittarius	♐	Jupiter	Jupiter
Capricorn	♑	Saturn	Saturn
Aquarius	♒	Saturn	Uranus
Pisces	♓	Jupiter	Neptune

Let us look at Sophie's data put together on Worksheet 2. We will be using the modern Rulers for this example.

Worksheet 2 for Sophie

Worksheet 2 for Sophie

Planet	Planet	Sign	Sign	Element	Mode	Ruler	Ruler's Sign	Element	Mode
☉	Sun	♏	Scorpio	Water	Fixed	♇	Leo	Fire	Fixed
☽	Moon	♒	Aquarius	Air	Fixed	♅	Cancer	Water	Card
☿	Mercury	♏	Scorpio	Water	Fixed	♇	Leo	Fire	Fixed
♀	Venus	♐	Sagittarius	Fire	Mut	♃	Taurus	Earth	Fixed
♂	Mars	♑	Capricorn	Earth	Card	♄	Libra	Air	Card
♃	Jupiter	♉	Taurus	Earth	Fixed	♀	Sagittarius	Fire	Mut
♄	Saturn	♎	Libra	Air	Card	♀	Sagittarius	Fire	Mut
♅	Uranus	♋	Cancer	Water	Card	☽	Aquarius	Air	Fixed
♆	Neptune	♎	Libra	Air	Card	♀	Sagittarius	Fire	Mut
♇	Pluto	♌	Leo	Fire	Fixed	☉	Scorpio	Water	Fixed
⚷	Chiron	♑	Capricorn	Earth	Card	♄	Libra	Air	Card
As	Asc	♎	Libra	Air	Card	♀	Sagittarius	Fire	Mut
Mc	MC	♌	Leo	Fire	Fixed	☉	Scorpio	Water	Fixed
☊	NNode	♒	Aquarius	Air	Fixed	♅	Cancer	Water	Card
☋	S Node	♌	Leo	Fire	Fixed	☉	Scorpio	Water	Fixed

Figure 17 - Worksheet 2 for Sophie

We then carry out the same procedure as before on Worksheet 1, of counting up the total number that each element appears and each mode appears.

Element	Total	Mode	Total
Fire	10	Cardinal	10
Earth	4	Fixed	15
Air	8	Mutable	5
Water	8		

Figure 17a - Element and Mode Totals for Sophie

The dominant element and mode for Sophie are Fire-10 / Fixed-15, which is associated with Leo

The weak combination here for Sophie is Earth - 4/Mutable-5, which relates to back to Virgo.

The disparity is more obvious with Worksheet 2. It gives us a clue to the underlying energies at play and it can produce a combination that is very different from Worksheet 1. In Sophie's case, Virgo remains the 'lacking' energy. The dominant energy in Worksheet 2 is the opposite and balance of the dominant energy in Worksheet 1. (Aquarius in

Worksheet 1, to Leo in Worksheet 2.) Neither is more 'right' than the other, they simply give different depths of view.

Leo and Virgo Biochemic Tissue Salts (Mag Phos and Kali Sulph) might be appropriate when working with Sophie's deep issues.

Similarly in the Bach Remedies, Leo and Virgo are connected with Vervain and Centaury. The element link of Earth, represented by Oak and the Mutable link represented by Wild Oat may also be worthy of consideration as they are identified as very low in the assessment.

Chapter 7

The Planets

The planets, Sun and Moon have been given correspondences to various organs and systems within the body. To gain the most from this sort of information some knowledge of how the body works is very helpful. Over the centuries the information has become part of our daily language as it has been introduced into common speech. Lunatic (associated with the Moon) and venereal (associated with Venus) are two examples we have adopted to do with health.

The simplest method to get a snapshot of where the energies of the planets concentrate their function for an individual can be done by creating a Body Overview (Appendix 6). This places the planets in the areas of the body designated by their signs, as shown in a natal chart.

Planet	Glyph	Organs	Body System	Type of Problem
Sun	☉	Heart, eyes	Immune system	Seasonal problems
Moon	☽	Body fluids	Lymphatic system	Fluctuation, monthly patterns
Mercury	☿	Thyroid	Nervous system, thought processes	Lack of self-expression creates stress
Venus	♀	Kidneys, thyroid	Hormonal system, glands	Self issues (self-worth, tolerance, acceptance
Mars	♂	Adrenals,	Reproductive system, muscles	Inflammation, injuries, Inability to express anger
Jupiter	♃	Liver	Left Brain, limbic system	Expansive, excessive,
Saturn	♄	Bones, teeth	Skeleton	Ageing, stiffening, blocks
Uranus	♅		Nervous systems	Spasms, sudden onset, tension
Neptune	♆	Pineal	Right Brain, Lymphatic system	Masks things, water retention, disperses energy
Pluto	♇	DNA	Cells growth	Chronic resistance to change
Chiron	⚷	Thymus gland	Immune system	Self sabotage

Figure 18 - Planets, Organs, Systems.
Using the Signs of the Zodiac to Define Where Planets Activate

For example: Using Sophie's data

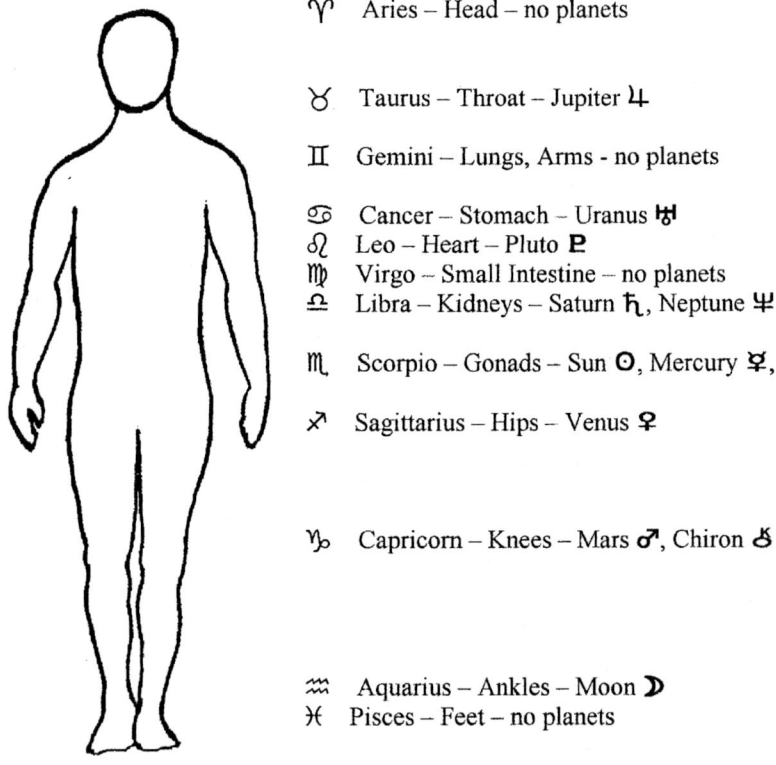

♈ Aries – Head – no planets

♉ Taurus – Throat – Jupiter ♃

♊ Gemini – Lungs, Arms - no planets

♋ Cancer – Stomach – Uranus ♅
♌ Leo – Heart – Pluto ♇
♍ Virgo – Small Intestine – no planets
♎ Libra – Kidneys – Saturn ♄, Neptune ♆

♏ Scorpio – Gonads – Sun ☉, Mercury ☿,

♐ Sagittarius – Hips – Venus ♀

♑ Capricorn – Knees – Mars ♂, Chiron ⚷

♒ Aquarius – Ankles – Moon ☽
♓ Pisces – Feet – no planets

Figure 19 - Body Overview for Sophie

From this straightforward plotting of a body overview, we could determine the following by matching the keywords of the signs of the zodiac with the type of energy indicated by each planet.

No Planets in Aries

Jupiter In Taurus
The throat needs to be expansive (Jupiter keyword), so its natural expression would be a need to communicate. If this was inhibited in any way, this area could quickly become troublesome.

No Planets In Gemini

Uranus in Cancer
Uranus in Cancer might suggest that Sophie could be prone to stomach cramps or unpredictable symptoms affecting the stomach.

Pluto in Leo
Pluto in Leo indicates the pressure to transform and understand how feelings can seriously affect her heart's health.

Saturn in Libra
Saturn in Libra focuses on the bones of the sacrum, suggesting that the older she gets the more she could suffer from stiffness here. Neptune in Libra suggests that difficulties could go undetected here and that she could benefit from ensuring that her kidneys are cared for by taking preventative measures such as drinking plenty of water and reducing stress levels where possible.

Sun in Scorpio
Sun in Scorpio focuses Sophie's life-force in her lower pelvis. Sun Scorpio shows an intense need to be creative, yet also

difficulties in being able to let go. Care to be taken then in avoiding constipation, bladder infections etc.

Mercury in Scorpio
Mercury in Scorpio suggests that she might be unwilling to talk about problems associated with her bowels, bladder and sexual organs.

Venus in Sagittarius
Venus in Sagittarius hints that she could be very aware of her hips, oversensitive in some way. High levels of fluid in the body might be evident from the thighs.

Mars in Capricorn
Mars in Capricorn suggests difficulties with knee joints. The knees also could be sites of lots of minor injuries and inflammation.

Chiron in Capricorn
Chiron adds to the Mars input, by creating a possibility concerning flexibility and/ or toxin build up around the knees.

Moon in Aquarius
The Moon in Aquarius emphasises the possibility of fluid collection or poor lymphatic drainage around the ankles.

For any individual, the planets and the signs combined in this way gives a basic understanding of how body functions or the focuses of certain functions have an affect on that person. It also provides a guideline for preventative action to maintain health. Areas and difficulties that could one day develop into more complex problems can be identified.

Using the Signs of the Zodiac to Determine How the Planets Work

Another way to combine planets and signs is to apply the energy of the signs of the zodiac to describe how a certain planet would work. This can then be related to the corresponding organ or body system. The correspondences associated with each organ or body system are most easily expressed on all levels. The emotions and thinking patterns could be thought of as the precursors of any physical difficulty experienced

This type of matching of planet and sign is closer to the usual type of delineation (putting information together in an understandable way) used in astrology.

For example:

For Sophie:

She has natal Sun in Scorpio.

The Sun (heart) would work in a Scorpio sort of way, prone to Scorpio-like difficulties and stresses, and create Scorpio-like problems when it is not functioning well.

Scorpio keywords could be listed as: intensely, emotionally, stubbornly, secretive, deep, powerful etc. It also relates to being capable in business, healing, research and looking at areas society would rather repress, such as sex, death, materialism.

Difficulties could arise for Sophie if she keeps deep emotions hidden. Stress builds up quickly when emotions have no release, or when there is a feeling of powerlessness. Scorpio (Fixed Water), unfortunately, is less likely to be flexible when dealing with emotions.

It is likely that she is very capable in a practical sort of way, but has problems when dealing with her emotions. With Mercury in Scorpio, there is little freedom to communicate about personal things, She probably spends a lot of time in thought, though not necessarily about personal issues (ironically, she may not be particularly aware of her own deep beliefs and thoughts). She probably assesses others well and would not think twice about using a very sharp tongue.

Moon in Aquarius combines the lunar cycle and emotions with the unpredictable energies of Aquarius. Body systems geared to the lunar cycle could be erratic - the menstrual cycle and lymphatic system. The instinctive emotions would tend to be detached, cool and she may feel that she doesn't seem to fit in with her surroundings, friends and family.

Venus in Sagittarius is open about relationships with a love of the exotic. Excessive self-indulgence could bring problems to this area, whether it is food or many lovers. The sense of self is likely to be well-developed and Sophie would not stint for her own comfort.

Mars in Capricorn needs to be in control in any situation and creates a lot of tension. Capricorn links to the skin and Mars to inflammation, so it is possible that skin complaints may occur when this aspect of her personality is thwarted in any way.

Generation Planets in Signs
The slower moving planets, like Jupiter, Saturn, Uranus, Neptune, Pluto and sometimes Chiron spend months or even years in certain signs. This shows how whole generations of people can manifest some similar, fundamental health patterns. These patterns occur on all levels, physical, emotional, mental and spiritual. It may be that looking back and taking an overview of each generation effect,

environmental and social factors may correlate with the specific signs that are prominent during those years.

A cycle of a planet is defined as the time it takes for that planet to complete one orbit around the Sun. During that time it will appear to pass through each sign of the zodiac in turn when it is viewed from the Earth. Jupiter, Saturn, Chiron and possibly also Uranus complete their cycles within a human lifetime. The cycles of Neptune and Pluto are so long that in our lifetimes we only experience parts of their cycle. The time that each planet appears in a sign varies. This depends on the distance the planet is from Earth. The effect of a combination of planet and sign is therefore, not only a personal one, but one that is shared in some way, with others born during the years when that combination occurred.

Jupiter

Jupiter cycle - approximately 12 years, spending a year in each sign. This planet indicates cycles of growth and development and is linked to the liver and to the learning processes of the logical left side of the brain. The manner of growth (on all levels), the response of the liver and ability to learn is indicated by the sign.

For Sophie, Jupiter in Taurus, shows slow but sure development and learning. Sophie's liver, one would expect to be sluggish and easily clogged by the effects of stress, infections or environmental pollution.

Saturn

Saturn cycle - approximately 28 years, spending just over 2 years in a sign. Saturn is linked to solidifying, so in all areas of health, it creates a lack of flexibility, stiffness and slowness of movement. On other levels it can show where there are blocks in emotions and thinking, where we like to control parts of our lives. For Sophie, Saturn is in Libra. This relates to the sacral area of the spine, with possible difficulties with kidneys and bladder.

Uranus

Uranus cycle - approximately 84 years, with the planet spending around 7 years in each sign. This planet shows the ability to break out of patterns, particularly those indicated by the sign it is in. It relates to innovation, new ideas and challenging the status quo. From a health angle, it represents spasmodic muscle activity and an inability to relax the mind and body. In Cancer (as in Sophie's chart), this reflects the changing role of the family that started as her generation reached adulthood. For her personally there could be food intolerances or problems with digestion when she doesn't relax enough.

Neptune

Neptune has a cycle that takes approximately 165 years to complete a cycle, spending around 13-14 years in a sign. An individual's experience of Neptune never includes a complete cycle. Fractions of the cycle especially at 26 years and 39 years often indicate years of a shift in personal values or lifestyle. Healthwise, these ages can pinpoint the start or end of underlying health problems that will undermine the life force of an individual. Neptune in Virgo (1928-1942) saw the beginning of the pharmaceutical industry, Virgo indicating the meticulous work that went on at those times. Ironically one of the healing techniques that subsequently nearly became lost to us with the advent of drugs, was the use of light. The gland most sensitive to light is the pineal, and only in the last few decades has its role in health been appreciated by orthodox medicine. The gland was thought to have no active role in modern man. Eventually research confirmed that this little gland situated in the centre of the head, was the control mechanism for establishing our daily rhythms. Neptune also represents psychism (also linked to the pineal through the famed 'Third Eye'), illusion and idealism. When Neptune was in Libra (1942-1956) it spawned the generation that went 'hippie' in the sixties, when love, recreational drugs and idealism was a dream that many shared. Personally, for someone like Sophie, with Neptune in Libra, the health triggers would pivot around partnership changes, or loss of ideals and is liable to centre in the lower back, kidney and bladder (water retention or infections).

Pluto

Pluto cycle has a full cycle of 265 years, spending approximately 22 years in a sign. Like Neptune, people experience only parts of the Pluto cycle, the most noted between 39 and 42 years, known as the 'mid-life crisis'. Pluto represents changes in the fundamental patterns of our lives, from the DNA in our cells to the spiritual drives in our souls. Each sign that Pluto occupies shows how every generation seeks to change the environment and themselves. Pluto in Cancer (1914-1939) saw the traditional family patterns being changed through the effect of World War I. Pluto in Leo (1939-1957) showed Man playing with explosive creation (the atom bomb), new attitudes to leaders and to individuals. Pluto in Virgo (1957- 1972), the generation to tidy up after the 'Leo' times and bring some order to the chaos of person-centred desires. Understanding of disease through the workings of the whole system. Pluto in Libra (1972- 1984) brought further transformation of partnerships and liberalisation of attitudes to sexuality.

On an individual level Pluto shows how we tackle our evolution and how we can release our full potential. For Sophie, with Pluto in Leo, this will be powerful release of creativity to bring about positive change for herself and those around her. If not touched on before the age of 39, these changes would be likely to disrupt her life considerably. Like the atom bomb explosions of the Second World War - things will never be quite the same.

Chiron

Chiron is a planetoid that was first spotted in our Solar System in 1977. It has a very elongated orbit, so that it spends a long time in some signs, and speeds quickly through others. It completes a cycle in 49-51 years. This marks a time for the individual when we meet the challenge to become who we really are. Quite often in the years moving up to this 'Chiron Return' all areas of our lives come under some sort of re-evaluation. Many astrologers feel it shows where we are 'wounded' and where, if we can explore what its sign placement indicates, we can begin to integrate and channel our disparate energies. Sophie's Chiron is in Capricorn. From a health angle, this indicates problems with knees, injuries and flexibility possibly associated with the immune system. She may have been made to feel that she would never succeed or feel secure (negative Capricorn), which thought patterns may have undermined. It may have encouraged constant attempts to achieve something or make something more of herself.

Chapter 8

Planets in Relationship to Each Other

When you have an accurate chart to work with, you can also explore how the planets and sensitive points relate to one another.

In astrology important relationships are measured as divisions of a circle. The mathematical measurement is made of segments of the circle, 360 in all, each one called a 'degree'. Certain numbers of degrees separating two points or planets have been found to show a special relationship between those planets or points. There are many of these types of relationships, called 'aspects', used in astrology, but here we will mention only four of the main ones and one especially linked to health.

Conjunction

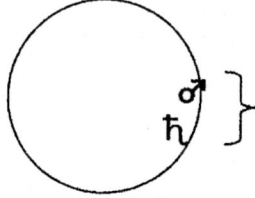

Figure 20 - Saturn Conjunct Mars

When planets or points are close together, within a range of 0-8 degrees apart, they are said to be 'conjunct' or 'in conjunction with' one another. Planets this close to each other have a direct effect on each other. The sort of effect depends on the nature of the planets involved and tends to exhibit both positive and negative qualities of the combination. To understand how they work together, you look at one set of meanings and marry them up to the other set.

For example:

If Saturn is conjunct Mars

	Saturn ♄	Mars ♂
Organ	Bones, teeth,	Adrenal Glands
System	Skeleton	Muscles
	Ageing, Stiffening, blocks	Inflammation, injuries
Emotion	Obstinate, conservative, slow	Impatient, Angry, restless
Type of energy	Steady, long-lasting	Immediate, short-lived

Figure 21 - Saturn / Mars Information

From this table, you can see initially that these two energies have little in common. As you begin to blend together the ideas from each, you could come up with things like:
- injuries to the bones
- strong muscles and bones

- frustration (slow versus impatient)
- inflammation to joints
- sluggish adrenal function
- good stamina

Whatever the energies in a 'Conjunction' the energies need to find ways to work together. If they are dissimilar, like Saturn and Mars, they will also aggravate each other too.

Opposition (Circle divided into two - 180 degrees)

When planets are opposite each other, within a variance, or 'orb', of 0 - 8 degrees, they are said to be in opposition. Here the planets have a relationship of polarity and tension. Unless just across the boundary or cusp, between signs, the planets will also be in opposite signs. The effect is rather like a see-saw, each vying for dominance or the upper hand. The effect on the individual depends on the planets involved, but most individuals easily recognise the experience of these negative combinations.

For example:

Jupiter opposition Moon

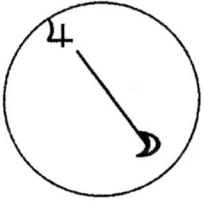

	Jupiter ♃	Moon ☽
Organ	Liver,	Body fluids
System	Left Brain	Lymphatic system
Emotion	Expansive	Sensitive, home-loving
Type of Energy	Excessive	Monthly cycle

Figure 23 - Jupiter/Moon Information

Like in the 'conjunction' these planets affect each other, but here they swing from one extreme to the other. You could have:
- excessive sensitivity to the moon cycle
- overbearing mothering
- headaches from fluid fluctuation in the brain
- clogged up liver and lymphatics due to living it up.

Trine (Circle divided into three - 120 degrees)

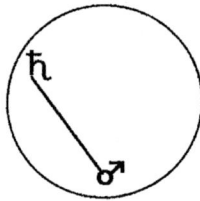

Figure 24 - Saturn Trine Mars

Here planets occur 120 degrees apart, usually also four signs apart, allowing an orb of 0 - 8 degrees. This relationship indicates an easy, positive flow of energy between the two.

As an example, lets take the Saturn and Mars table.

	Saturn ♄	Mars ♂
Organ	Bones, teeth,	Adrenal Glands
System	Skeleton	Muscles
	Ageing, Stiffening, blocks	Inflammation, injuries
Emotion	Obstinate, conservative, slow	Impatient, Angry, restless
Type of energy	Steady, long-lasting	Immediate, short-lived

Figure 25 / Figure 21 - Saturn / Mars Information

If these energies were working in a 'trine' relationship, you could create the following ideas, by looking at the positive ways the two energies help each other:

- exercise easily helps to keep bones healthy
- ability to control anger
- ability to rest
- good stamina
- careful activity avoids injuries

Square (Circle divided into four - 90 degrees)

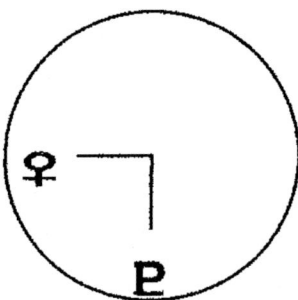

Figure 26 - Venus Square Pluto

The planets that have a 'square relationship' are 90 degrees or three signs apart (allowing 0 - 8 degrees orb). Planets in this type of relationship create an inner conflict, which is released by taking action or creating movement of some sort. This can be seen as negative, in that conflict and stress is experienced, or as positive, an effort is made to resolve the conflict and so creates movement and the possibility of change.

An example could be Venus and Pluto

	Venus ♀	Pluto ♇
Organ	Kidneys, Thyroid	DNA
System	Hormones	Cell growth
Emotion	Self issues	Resistance to change
Type of Energy	Relating, creating	Transformation

Figure 27 - Venus/Pluto Information

In a 'square' relationship, these two bring to mind:

- self issues need to be explored and worked with
- possible thyroid and kidney problems creating problems with physical appearance
- reproductive difficulties creating a change in how creativity and relationships are expressed.

Quincunx or Inconjunct (a fraction of the circle - 5/ 12)

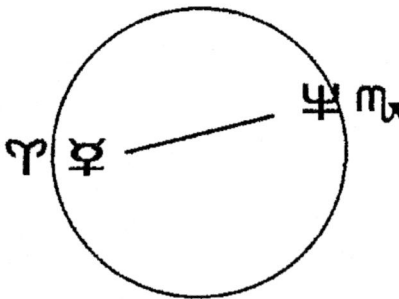

Figure 28 - Aries Mercury Quincunx Scorpio Neptune

This aspect occurs with planets or sensitive points that are 150 degrees or five signs apart. The leeway on this type of interrelationship is only 3 degrees either way. This aspect is a difficult one to work with from any angle, health or otherwise. It often shows habit patterns that are difficult to break or health issues that persist in some form, no matter how much healing is applied.

	Mercury ☿	Neptune ♆
Organ	Thyroid	Pineal
System	Nervous, Thinking	Lymphatic
Emotion	Expression	Illusion, idealism
Type of Energy	Information flow	Masks, disperses

Figure 29 - Mercury / Neptune Information

In a quincunx relationship these two planets could indicate:

- disruption of sleeping patterns
- weight increase
- woolly thinking
- inability to communicate clearly

However, certain signs involved in this 150 degree relationship have correspondences to the meridians of Traditional Chinese Medicine. When planets occur in these signs with the quincunx aspect to each other, they emphasise the role of those meridians in the fundamental health of the individual. This can be useful information to share with an acupuncturist, shiatsu practitioner or kinesiologist.

Sign	Meridian	Sign	Meridian	5-Element	4-Element
Aries	Kidney	Scorpio	Bladder	Water	Water
Gemini	Liver	Capricorn	Gall Bladder	Wood	Air
Virgo	Large Intestine	Aquarius	Lung	Metal	Earth
Cancer	Stomach	Sagittarius	Spleen	Earth	Earth
Taurus	Triple Heater/Warmer	Libra	Heart Protector	Fire	Fire
Leo	Heart	Pisces	Small Intestine	Fire	Fire

Figure 30 - Correspondences between the Signs of the Zodiac and the Meridians of Traditional Chinese Medicine

Ascendant
With an accurate chart, the Ascendant needs to be looked at carefully. The Ascendant is often taken to represent the body of a person, so planets in particular aspects to the Ascendant will have special bearing on health.

Traditionally Saturn and Mars in any aspect to the Ascendant would have bearing on the health. Mars, indicative of the level or quality of life-force the person has and Saturn hinting at longevity and the quality of life in later years.

Any planet will bring its own vibrational quality to the situation. Simply put, the planets could bring the following:

The Sun will bring warmth, outgoing nature and confidence also seasonal complaints

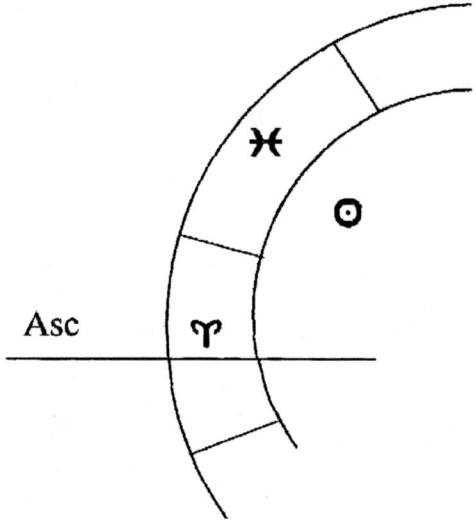

Figure 31- Ascendant

The Moon brings sensitivity, nurturing and caring, also fluid problems with the moon-cycle.

Mercury emphasises communication, adaptability and versatility also nervousness and inability to relax.

Venus, amplifies attractiveness, allure and creativity, also hormone problems and difficulties with acceptance of self.

Mars brings energy, daring and action and also inflammation and a predisposition for minor accidents.

Jupiter exaggerates all it touches, bigger, louder and faster so health problems will tend to arise as a result of excesses.

Saturn gives a serious flavour; persistence, maturity, steadiness but also joint stiffness.

Chiron gives an unpredictable quality and a need to heal the self but also a knack of wrecking that very same process.

The so-called 'generation' planets of Uranus, Neptune and Pluto take on a very personal significance when in close aspect to the Ascendant. ('Close aspect' meaning that the degree measurement of the Ascendant and planet concerned are with 8 degrees of each other.)

Uranus highlights the unusual, eccentricity, intuition and rebellion, also muscle pain and tension.

Neptune brings psychism, sensitivity, artistry, healing skills, illusion, also problems with drugs and water retention.

Pluto shows that personal power needs careful use as it transforms and changes. It also brings resistance to change even if it will be of benefit.

Planets in close conjunction to the Ascendant are often associated with the actual birth and its circumstances. Playing with the meaning of the planets and the sign of the Ascendant can bring helpful insights to the moment of birth and the subsequent patterns of health.

For example, Uranus close to the Ascendant could indicate a sudden, unexpected or very quick birth. It might also suggest birth during unusual circumstances - like a thunderstorm.

Chapter 9

Healing Strategies Using Astrology

Biochemic Tissues Salts and the Bach Flower Remedies are excellent tools to use in combination with astrological data that is derived from the signs of the zodiac and how they are emphasised for each person.

Healing tools related to the planets can be introduced where one or more of the planets is shown to have an important role in the health and well-being of a person.

Sun
Where the Sun is involved, you need to become aware of the cycle of the seasons. Try to become aware of which seasons you like and dislike. When you can identify or isolate particular times, plan ahead. When those times of the year approach ensure you have your back-up remedies, supports and strategies already prepared.

For example, if you know you always feel low in the early part of the year or you get glum in the autumn- check out the lighting at home and work. Ideally you need full-spectrum light (similar to light from the sun which contains all the colours of the spectrum). If that is not possible, consider getting a light box. You could change some light-bulbs for blue craft-lights (available from art shops) or quartz lighting. Avoid fluorescent lighting and the looped type of long-life bulb as they give off only a fraction of the light spectrum you need.

If it always the same month - check the zodiac sign for that month and take the Biochemic Tissue Salt or Bach Flower Remedy for that sign.

Moon

When the Moon is involved, the cycle experienced is much smaller - every 28 days. You don't need to be female to experience a monthly cycle! Start by watching the Moon at night. Note how you feel at new, full and dark moons. If you recognise disruptions occur at the same time each month, then awareness that you are in for a few delicate days helps to ease you through the experience.

If you notice a monthly cycle that is not to do with the moon phases then you need to look at an ephemeris (planetary tables). Check here, to see if sensitivity is always when the Moon is in a particular sign of the zodiac. Again, forewarned is forearmed.

Since the Moon is related to the lymphatic system of the body it might be worth adding essential fatty acids, like Evening Primrose Oil and fish oils to the diet. These supplements are important keys to the provision of steady energy for many tissues within the body, lack of fatty acids can have a marked effect on swinging moods.

Mercury

If Mercury is involved the cycle is harder to determine as it does not fit in to an easy number of months, taking 88 days to complete its orbit. Symptoms to look for are the inability to relax, both physically and mentally. Finding it hard to get to sleep because your mind won't stop is a pretty good indicator of a Mercury influence. Taking a leaf out of philosophies from the East may help. We in the West put a lot of emphasis on the workings of the mind and often get confused about the part it plays in our lives. We say 'my mind this...... my mind that.....' indicating that we do know it is something separate from 'us'. Yet we treat its influence into our lives with more importance than maybe we should. The mind should not rule us. We should be the 'master' and it the 'servant'. Yet when Mercury affects our well-being, quite often the 'servant' is in control. Taking time out to rest helps, even if you need to set an alarm clock, not to wake you up, but to ensure you physically stay in one place for say - 20 minutes. Listening to music helps, sometimes a guided visualisation spoken by someone else helps (on a tape, for example).

People write and talk about quietening the mind. This is impossible for most of us, and after all, the nature of the mind is constant movement and activity, so trying to quieten it will always be singularly unsuccessful. What we can try to do is not to be distracted by the movement of our thoughts. This does not mean trying to police our minds into silence! It means sitting still and allowing thoughts to be - with no attempt to control them, no attempt to label or follow them. Even doing this for a minute or two can create more peace in your day.

Venus

Venus energy is related to the views we hold about ourselves and the world around us. Wise people tell us that the world we create for ourselves in our minds is the world we live our lives in. For example, if we think of ourselves in a critical way, it affects the way we relate to others. This in turn creates patterns of lost opportunity, which reinforces the critical beliefs we hold about ourselves - and so on. Negative belief patterns can also form the foundation for health issues of all sorts, from the simple to the very complex. Venus shows the need to re-create positive beliefs for ourselves.

Writers such as John Diamond, Louise Hay and Stuart Wilde have explained to us how we can go about changing our thoughts. Louise Hay and Stuart Wilde take the approach of identifying a positive phrase and then repeating it may times, gradually changing the fundamental thinking pattern.

John Diamond takes this a step further. Recognising that our bodies know by energy changes when we lie to ourselves, he suggests ways to allow new beliefs by using careful muscle testing and gentle activation of meridian points that can re-programme our bodies to accept and work with positive beliefs.

Physical therapies like massage, aromatherapy and reflexology, can be very useful to augment poor self-image and lack of value in the self and body. Receiving these types of therapies allows us to accept positive attention from other people. Gradually this can help us to be more accepting of ourselves. Paying money to someone else to give us this sort of attention also helps us to value it. There is though, a fine line between paying someone because we value their input and paying someone because we have become too dependant or too lazy to do make the effort for ourselves.

Mars
If Mars is implicated, activity needs to be undertaken to ensure that the energy it creates has a positive and creative outlet. Energy is only experienced as negative, when it is expressed inappropriately. Anger is a good example. Anger as an emotion is not negative it is a healthy response to certain situations. It becomes negative when it is expressed in a dangerous way, or when it is repressed. It doesn't go away when it is repressed, it just 'does its thing' by damaging the internal functioning of the person in some way.

Mars often needs some sort of practical activity to be undertaken in order to release its force and restore equilibrium. Such activity does not need to make you break out into perspiration. Good exercise is gentle and involves all the body, like yoga, Tai chi or swimming. If the chosen activity can be creative, like gardening, it can give an expression to Mars energy that can be appreciated and shared by others.

Jupiter

Helping to relieve Jupiter problems means looking at our lives to see where we indulge ourselves. This can bring us to areas where we go over-the-top as a form of comfort, or where we genuinely really like something, but don't know where to draw the line on sensible use. This can be in any area of our lives, even in the workplace!

Dealing with Jupiter means reining in or learning to control ourselves before real health damage occurs. Where liver function is under par, whether due to exhaustion, infection or indulgence, herbs seem to be one the best methods to bring back a healthy balance. True to Jupiter energy though, some of the excesses we are liable to enjoy might well create liver problems in the long term. Some just create a bigger waistline, bigger holes in teeth, or and create more weight to ignore on the bathroom scales!

Jupiter, when associated with growth, is linked to vitamins. Vitamins are minute amount of certain nutrients that cannot be made in sufficient amounts by the body, so have to come from our food. Without good quality food we are unable to get the right amount of nutrients required for growth and health. Good quality food doesn't mean lots of food. Good food is chemical-free, organic and fresh, that benefits us and the planet we live on.

Saturn

Problems linked with Saturn require us to keep our joints flexible and our bones strong. Osteopathy, chiropractic, physiotherapy and other body-manipulation techniques can be helpful. Linked closely to Saturn are the difficulties that develop due to age and wear and tear on our bodies. Any part of our body that becomes immobile due to stiffness or injury, will be under the influence of Saturn. Our ability to cope with and repair this can depend on the mineral intake from our foods, (also from items like the Biochemic Tissue Salts).

Uranus

People with strong Uranian energy find it very hard to relax. Here the simple techniques useful for Mercury may prove to be inadequate. Blending relaxation and meditation with dancing and music may help to get the Uranus energy earthed. Traditionally Uranus has been associated with people who can combine all their skills to work ceremonial healings. Drumming, didgeridoo and other deep-noted rhythmical sounds often bring the body's core energy to a level that it can be used. Like Neptune, learning about core shamanic techniques, and other earth-based skills can release powerful healing abilities.

Neptune

Neptune energy does not need to work away from the physical earth, like in visualisations, imaginations or mind-based skills. All of these come naturally to someone with a strong Neptune. The challenge is to earth the skill and to make it of practical use to yourself and those around you.

Often the desire is to escape this planet, or to expect someone to rescue you from the horrors of living, when you really need to get stuck into the nitty-grittys of everyday life. Avoid drugs (prescribed pharmaceutical, recreational and social) if you can. Get Real! Get your hands dirty! Don't avoid the nasty bits! This doesn't make the imagination, the sensitivity and the creativity go away. On the contrary, it gives you an effective means to use, manage and express Neptune energy in the world.

Pluto

When Pluto is strong in the chart or highlighted in some way there is an issue somewhere within the personality about how to use power wisely. Whether it expresses through willpower, destruction, transformation or creation, it brings with it changes that affect the whole of the life. Like DNA it remains locked inside, buried most of the time. When it activates, it is important to realise the change it brings is inevitable. With hindsight it is usually easy to see it working. When you are experiencing it, the need to move with the change is not so obvious, the change is not so visible.

When your life seems to be crashing in around your or you are stubbornly resisting change. Stop. Think about what is going on. What are you really afraid of? What do you want to keep the same?

Cells have a limited lifetime. They need to die for new cells to replace them. Without this cycle of life and death, the organism dies. Without change, without transformation, we may not die, but we don't grow. Maybe a spark of life inside dies.

Chiron

From the mythology associated with Chiron, it indicates where we have health problems that, as we work with them and try to relieve them we learn more and more about ourselves. What we learn, we can then use to help others. The sign of Chiron will give a clue to the type of difficulties we are liable to encounter. All we need to do is to explore ways of dealing with Chiron's difficulties as they present themselves.

Chapter 10

Example of an Astrology Healing Assessment

This is the astrological information for Robert (We have an accurate chart available see Figure 32)

From this we can assess that Robert has a dominance of Water-6 / Cardinal-7 and Water-6 / Mutable-6. This translates to the influence of Cancer and Pisces

He is lacking in Air -2 / Fixed- 2 - which translates back to Aquarius.

Assessing for the Biochemic Tissue Salts, this would equate to Calc Fluor (Cancer), Ferr Phos (Pisces) and Nat Mur (Aquarius).

These salts pinpoint possible difficulties with the connective tissues, circulation and inflammation.

Looking at the Bach Flower Remedies, the Twelve Healers, this pattern would equate to a mixture of Rock Rose (Cancer), Clematis (Pisces) and Water Violet (Aquarius). These would suggest Robert is attached to the past, fearful, escapist and distant.

Figure 32 – Robert's Astrological Chart

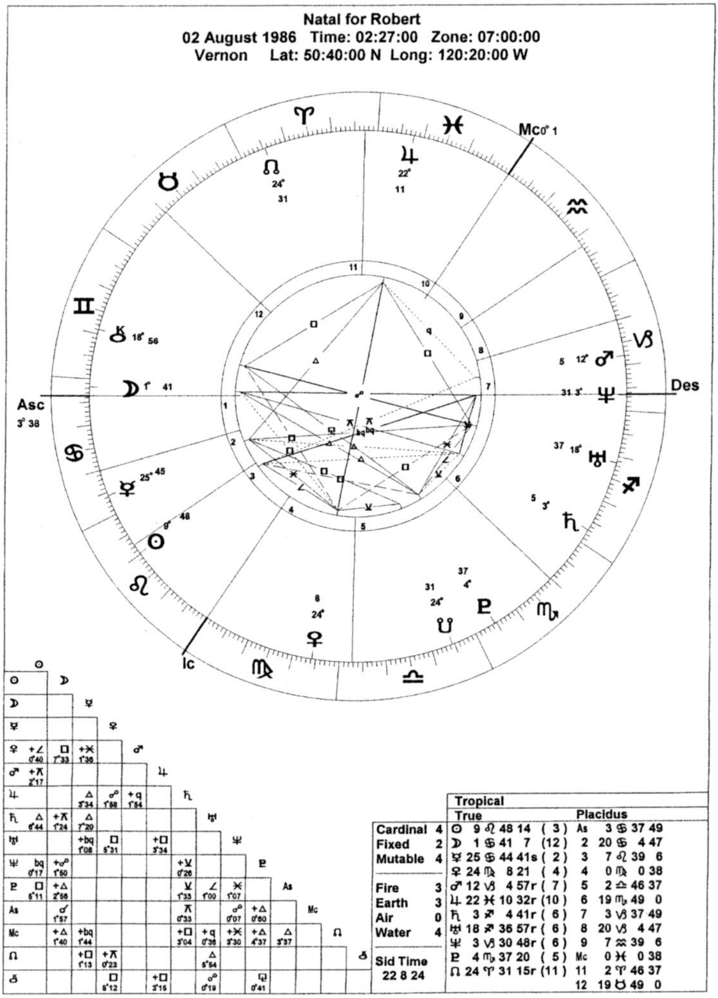

Worksheet 1 for Robert

Planet	Planet	Sign	Sign	Element	Mode of Action
☉	Sun	Leo	♌	Fire	Fixed
☽	Moon	Cancer	♋	Water	Cardinal
☿	Mercury	Cancer	♋	Water	Cardinal
♀	Venus	Virgo	♍	Earth	Mutable
♂	Mars	Capricorn	♑	Earth	Cardinal
♃	Jupiter	Pisces	♓	Water	Mutable
♄	Saturn	Sagittarius	♐	Fire	Mutable
♅	Uranus	Sagittarius	♐	Fire	Mutable
♆	Neptune	Capricorn	♑	Earth	Cardinal
♇	Pluto	Scorpio	♏	Water	Fixed
⚷	Chiron	Gemini	♊	Air	Mutable
As	Ascendant	Cancer	♋	Water	Cardinal
Mc	Midheaven	Pisces	♓	Water	Mutable
☊	North Node	Aries	♈	Fire	Cardinal
☋	South Node	Libra	♎	Air	Cardinal

Element	Element Totals	Mode	Mode Totals
Fire	4	Cardinal	7
Earth	3	Fixed	2
Air	2	Mutable	6
Water	6		

Figure 33 - Worksheet 1 for Robert

Considering the Seven Helpers, Air (2) and Fixed (2) stand out as possibilities, so Heather (Air) and Olive (Fixed) might also be helpful. These could suggest Robert need to communicate a lot, yet he can be stubborn and may lack confidence.

If we then apply Robert's data to Worksheet 2, for a deeper look.

From Worksheet 2 Robert's dominant energies are Water-14/Cardinal-11. This is directly associated with the sign of Cancer Its Biochemic Tissue Salt is Calc. Fluor and Bach Flower Remedy, Rock Rose.

The lacking energy is Air-2/Fixed -4. This relates to Aquarius. The Biochemic Tissue Salt is Nat. Mur and Bach Flower Remedy is Water Violet.

Worksheet 2 for Robert

Planet	Planet	Sign	Sign	Element	Mode	Ruler	Ruler's Sign	Element	Mode
☉	Sun	Leo	♌	Fire	F	☉	Leo	Fire	F
☽	Moon	Cancer	♋	Water	C	☽	Cancer	Water	C
☿	Mercury	Cancer	♋	Water	C	☽	Cancer	Water	C
♀	Venus	Virgo	♍	Earth	M	☿	Cancer	Water	C
♂	Mars	Capricorn	♑	Earth	C	♄	Sagittarius	Fire	M
♃	Jupiter	Pisces	♓	Water	M	♆	Capricorn	Earth	C
♄	Saturn	Sagittarius	♐	Fire	M	♃	Pisces	Water	M
♅	Uranus	Sagittarius	♐	Fire	M	♃	Pisces	Water	M
♆	Neptune	Capricorn	♑	Earth	C	♄	Sagittarius	Fire	M
♇	Pluto	Scorpio	♏	Water	F	♇	Scorpio	Water	F
⚷	Chiron	Gemini	♊	Air	M	☿	Cancer	Water	C
As	Asc	Cancer	♋	Water	C	☽	Cancer	Water	C
Mc	MC	Pisces	♓	Water	M	♆	Capricorn	Earth	C
☊	NNode	Aries	♈	Fire	C	♂	Capricorn	Earth	C
☋	S Node	Libra	♎	Air	C	♀	Virgo	Earth	M

Element	Element Totals	Mode	Mode Totals
Fire	7	Cardinal	15
Earth	7	Fixed	4
Air	2	Mutable	11
Water	14		

Figure 34 - Worksheet 2 for Robert

The assessment from Worksheet 1 highlighted Cancer, Pisces and Aquarius. Worksheet 2 has created a tighter focus on the two signs Cancer and Aquarius.

Looking at the Planets

From the Body Overview

Chiron in Gemini (lungs, arms) could suggest that a weakening of the immune system could come into the body via the lungs, or maybe by touching something. It also indicates problems with the upper back may occur that are difficult to resolve.

Moon and Mercury in Cancer highlight the pivotal role of the stomach and how emotions and worries easily upset digestion.

Venus in Virgo links to many aspects of digestion and assimilation of food. The pancreas and small intestine supply important enzymes and digestive hormones that may dysfunction when stressed. Virgo also rules the liver, hinting that stress to do with attitudes about himself or his body might complicate the liver's ability to manage to keep the chemical balance correct.

Sun in Leo confirms Robert has a strong constitution with a high level of life-force and fundamentally strong immune system. It would take a debilitating illness to weaken him.

Pluto in Scorpio indicates that the ability of the body to release its waste is crucial to allow healing to occur.

Saturn in Sagittarius can create stiffness in the hips and energy blocks in the thighs. Uranus in Sagittarius aggravates

The Body Overview for Robert

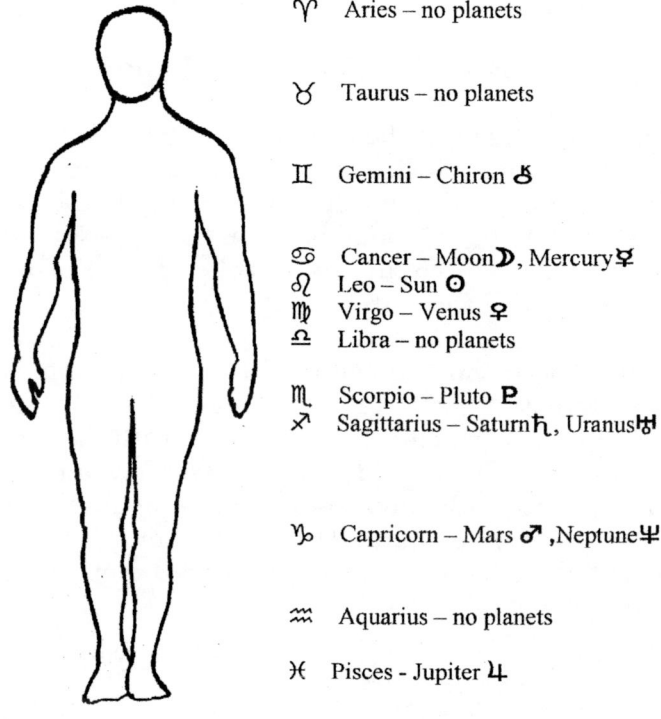

♈ Aries – no planets

♉ Taurus – no planets

♊ Gemini – Chiron ⚷

♋ Cancer – Moon ☽, Mercury ☿
♌ Leo – Sun ☉
♍ Virgo – Venus ♀
♎ Libra – no planets

♏ Scorpio – Pluto ♇
♐ Sagittarius – Saturn ♄, Uranus ♅

♑ Capricorn – Mars ♂, Neptune ♆

♒ Aquarius – no planets

♓ Pisces - Jupiter ♃

Figure 35 - Body Overview for Robert

this with tension and muscle spasms likely in the hip and thigh area, or the lower back, that creates pain in the hips.

Mars in Capricorn indicates injuries and inflammation of the knees. Neptune present here suggests that knee problems may mask other difficulties and may be a source of weakening (dispersing energy).

Jupiter in Pisces hints at swelling in the feet and liver problems subsequently affecting the feet in some way.

Blending Robert's Signs of the Zodiac with the Planets

Robert's Sun is in Leo, one of the most powerful places for the Sun to be. This confirms his strong drive to live, strong levels of life-force and a firm sense of self. Stress would build up if Robert were unable to be outgoing, be seen, be appreciated or if he felt unwanted. He could easily take charge of any situation and be quite authoritative.

His Moon is in Cancer, shows great sensitivity and caring, not always easily compatible with a Leo Sun sign. The lymphatic system will fluctuate as will all the body fluids, with the lunar cycle. All fluid activity in the body will ebb and flow and will need careful nurturing. Mercury present here highlights the thyroid, which will also fluctuate in the way it functions. With either of these, loss of nurturing, through poor diet or poor emotional support will affect the health.

Venus in Virgo confirms that the thyroid and kidney functioning is tightly tied into the levels of mental stress. Virgo is a 'perfectionist' type of energy, so effort is put into activities to achieve perfection in some way. When events don't go as planned the thyroid, kidneys and hormones would take the brunt of the mental stress. This type of placement also occurs with people who are hyperactive and workaholic.

Pluto in Scorpio links to the way people of Robert's generation react to their environment. The necessary change needed to progress or move away from deeply held issues is slow and difficult.

Saturn in Sagittarius is control (Saturn) working on an outgoing energy (Sagittarius). where Robert wishes to explore and expand. Progress may be slower than anticipated and create frustration.

Uranus in Sagittarius aggravates the physical difficulties likely with hips and thighs. On other levels, though, it could bring unexpected opportunities and adventures.

Mars in Capricorn manages energy well, but creates tension and inflammation in the knees. If achievement is prevented, the knees and/or the skin may show the effects. Neptune here, creates illusion or masks the real problems. Robert would need to be aware that if knee difficulties occur other factors may be the real cause.

Jupiter in Pisces is an expansive, creative energy. Its links with the liver suggest that anything in excess could affect liver function.

Chiron in Gemini hints at the lungs could be an area that might induce healing crises through ingestion of airborne pollutants or sensitivity to air quality . It also suggests that more than one route to healing may be needed as Gemini has traditionally been associated with two (as in Gemini, The Twins).

Some Key aspects within Robert's chart

Robert's Ascendant is conjunct the Moon, increasing the already high levels of sensitivity indicated by the sign of Cancer. It might also suggest an exploration of the circumstances at birth might shed light on susceptibility to certain types of health problems. The Ascendant is also opposition Neptune, hinting further that some sensitivity may have been created by anaesthetics or something similar during the birth process. Ascendant trine Pluto confirms a lot going on to create change to transform the situation from birth.

Venus is opposition Jupiter showing a tension between the kidneys, thyroid and the liver function and also between the hormone system and certain brain functions. This might suggest that if one area has a problem it will set up a see-sawing effect with the other organs.

There is an exact quincunx from the Ascendant to Saturn in Sagittarius. These two signs relate to the meridians Stomach and Spleen of Traditional Chinese Medicine. The precision of this relationship emphasises the central role that these meridians have in the maintenance of Robert's health. The Stomach meridian relates to contentment and tranquillity and is associated with hunger and disappointment. The Spleen meridian relates to faith in or anxiety about, the future and is associated with real concerns about forthcoming events. These correspondences are liable to play in Robert's life.

About Robert

Robert is a very active and able teenager who has experienced environmental pesticide poisoning. The most obvious of the symptoms included loss of body mass, rampant appetite and a need for constant physical activity. Orthodox approaches failed to deal with these issues. The diagnoses ranged from bulimia or anorexia to child abuse.

From the viewpoint of alternative healing, the toxicity seemed to have settled deep into the tissues and nerves. This affected the nerves and muscles, producing variable aches and joint problems. The biochemistry was disrupted, the neurotransmitters within the endocrine (hormonal) system creating many of the bizarre symptoms. These in turn affected the behaviour, similar to autism. As well as these difficult symptoms there was the practical problem of a food bill that would provide for a small army.

As often happens when a person becomes quite ill, the symptoms gravitate towards the key organs and systems highlighted by the natal chart. After the event, these are all too apparent. For all of us though, it emphasises the importance of knowing our strengths and weaknesses as shown by a natal chart assessment. This enables us to act in a preventative way, avoiding the weaknesses being augmented to create disease. As in this case, a lot of misspent energy, worry anxiety can be lessened or avoided altogether.

From the assessments came the following information:

Biochemic Tissue Salts - Calc Fluor and Nat Mur came up in Worksheet 1 and 2. Calc Fluor relates to connective tissues, blood vessel walls, Nat Mur, with circulation, and fluid problems. These were relevant to Robert's case as the toxicity affected all the systems indicated.

Bach Flower Remedies Rock Rose and Water Violet would help with his extreme sensitivity and Robert's experience that the practicalities of the problems meant it was difficult to become part of the social scene.

The Body Overview highlighted the areas of Robert's body most affected and explains the seemingly unrelated symptoms that were occurring.

The 'planets in signs' for Robert confirmed the remarkably strong constitution that has seen him through all of this. It also explained why, for example, the knee, hip and thigh aches have persisted (Saturn and Uranus in Sagittarius, Mars and Neptune in Capricorn). They also highlighted his sensitivity. In hindsight (a wonderful thing!), if the astrological information had been available, his contacts with chemicals of all sorts may have consciously been kept to a minimum.His natal astrological chart showed key relationships between planets that help to explain his predisposition to the whole episode.

His healing journey began with a homeopath. Sensing the gravity of the situation the homeopath asked for input from a kinesiologist who specialised in difficult cases. This was the first confirmation the family had had that chemical poisoning could be at the root of the problem. Prior to that more conventional approaches had suggested psychological or family problems as the cause.

Traditional Chinese Medicine had correctly identified the Stomach/Spleen meridians as a problem, but even daily acupuncture failed to bring much relief as Robert's system was too stressed to respond. Slowly, with herbs, flower essences, vitamins and minerals, Robert began to pull out. Chance contact with the book *'Molecules of Emotion'* by Candace Pert[6] brought in close scrutiny of the role of the digestive neurotransmitter CCK (Cholecystokokin). Through kinesiology, this was subtly adjusted successfully. The next big step forward for Robert came with contact with a classical osteopath, who gently encouraged the deep tissues in the body to release the pesticide. The osteopath confirmed the affect on the thyroid, liver and knees. Other forms of energy medicine continue to aid the detoxifying process and have helped Robert to alleviate the worst of the symptoms and to begin to be part of the normal teenage scene.

Footnote

6- *'Molecules of Emotion'* by Dr Candace Pert published by Simon and Schuster 1997. ISBN 0-684-81981-3.
CCK information on pages 182-184

Chapter 11

Further Explorations with Transits

There are many routes that can expand the way that you can assess health and modes of healing from the chart. Of the two presented in the following chapters, one is a standard 'next step' and the other an interesting and helpful approach for when someone is starting on their spiritual path or has met a spiritual crisis on the way.

Transits

The natal astrological chart is a snapshot of the positions of the Sun, Moon and planets as they appeared at the exact time of birth, viewed from the place of birth.

The planets are of course, in continual movement. Over the passage of time the moving planets will themselves enter into new relationships or create new aspects with the planets of the natal chart.

'Transit' is the name given to this natural passage of planets through the signs of the zodiac.

For example, if we look at Sophie's birth chart and compare her birth chart with the movement of planets on September 30th 1998.

Sophie had been under the weather, with minor, irritating and sometimes debilitating symptoms for over a year. However, this was the day when she realised and accepted that she was not well and needed to take some sort of action to resolve or deal with the situation.

The ephemeris (planetary tables) for that time shows:

If we copy the positions of these planets onto the outer edge of Sophie's chart, we can then start to look at the information that can be gleaned.

Sun	Moon	N.Node	Merc.	Venus	Mars	Jup.	Saturn	Uranus	Neptune	Pluto	Chiron
7Li7	25Cp41	29Le18	10Li45	29Vi25	25Le41	21Pi12	1Ta56	8Aq57	29Cp25	5Sg52	18Sc54

Figure 36 - Ephemeris for 30th September 1998

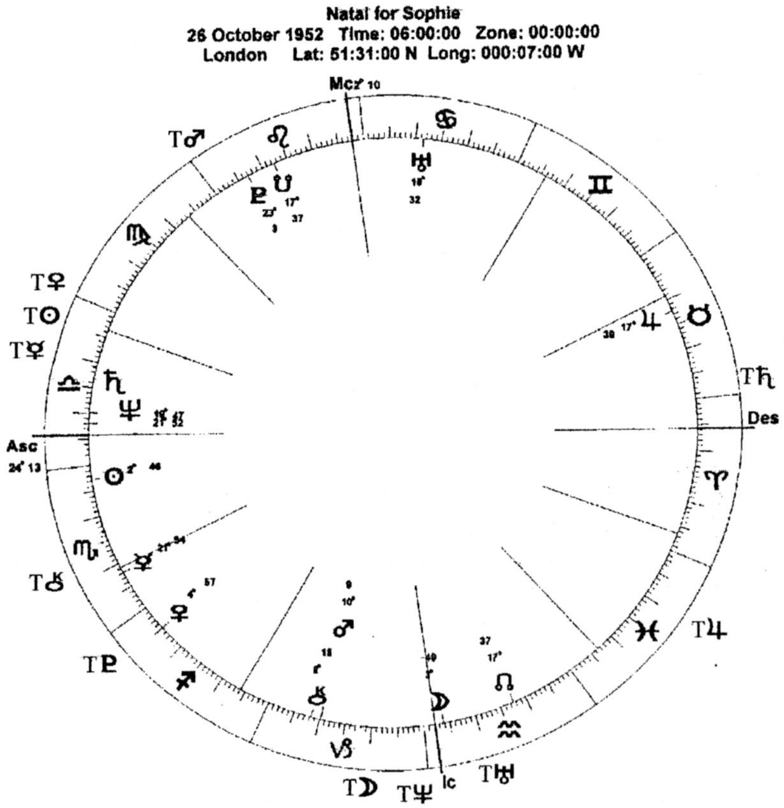

Figure 37 - Transits Around Sophie's Chart

Taking the transiting planets, one at a time, calculations are made to see if they create any aspects (conjunction, opposition, trine, square or quincunx) with the planets in her natal chart.

The amount of leeway of each aspect (orb) would be about three degrees for a sharp focus or up to six degrees for a more general focus.

For Sophie, we will take a sharp focus, and look for aspects that occur three degrees either side of the exact value of each aspect.

Conjunction (0 degrees)
Opposition (180 degrees)
Trine (120 degrees)
Square (90 degrees)
Quincunx (150 degrees)

If the transiting planet is between 28-29 degrees of a sign, or 1-2 degrees of a sign, we need to check aspects across the boundaries or cusps of the bordering signs.

For the astrologers amongst you, wondering about other aspects, for this exercise we are staying with the aspects mentioned earlier in the book.

Transiting Sun
Transiting Sun is at 7 degrees Libra, so we need to look for planets and points that range between 4 and 10 degrees of any sign.

Looking around Sophie's natal chart at the degrees of planets, we note:

Venus is at 4 degrees Sagittarius, creating an angle 60 degrees (a sextile aspect in astrology, but an aspect we are not using for this exercise).

Mars is 10 degrees Capricorn creating an aspect of 90 degrees, a square.

Moon
We know the Moon moves through a sign, every 2 and a half days, so for the purposes of this type of health assessment, we will ignore the Moon as it will make lots of contacts.

Transiting Mercury
Mercury is at 10 degrees Libra, so we look for planets between 7 and 13 degrees of any sign.

Mars is at 10 degrees Capricorn creating an aspect of 90 degrees, a square.

Transiting Venus
Venus is at 29 degrees Virgo, so we look for planets between 26 and 2 degrees of any sign.

The Sun is at 2 degrees Scorpio, creating an angle of 30 degrees (a semi-sextile aspect in astrology which we are not using for this exercise).

Midheaven is at 2 degrees Leo, creating an angle of 60 degrees.

Transiting Mars
Mars is at 25 degrees Leo, so we look for planets between 22 and 28 degrees in any sign.

Pluto is at 23 degrees Leo creating a conjunction.

Ascendant is at 24 degrees Libra, creating an angle of 60 degrees.

Transiting Jupiter
Jupiter is at 21 degrees Pisces, so we look for planets at 18 to 24 degrees in any sign.

Mercury is at 21 degrees Scorpio creating an aspect of 120 degrees, a trine.

Saturn is at 19 degrees Libra creating an aspect of 150 degrees, a quincunx.

Uranus is at 18 degrees Cancer, creating an aspect of 120 degrees, a trine.

Neptune is at 21 degrees Libra creating an aspect of 150 degrees, a quincunx.

Ascendant is at 24 degrees Libra creating an aspect of 150 degrees, a quincunx.

Transiting Saturn
Saturn is at 1 degree Taurus, so we look for planets from 28 to 4 degrees in any sign.

Sun is at 2 degrees Scorpio creating an aspect of 180 degrees, an opposition.

Moon is at 3 degrees Aquarius creating an aspect of 90 degrees, a square.

Venus is at 4 degrees Sagittarius creating an aspect of 150 degrees, a quincunx.

Midheaven is at 2 degrees Leo creating an aspect of 90 degrees, a square.

Transiting Uranus
Uranus is at 8 degrees Aquarius, so we look for planets from 5 degrees to 11 degrees.

Mars is at 10 degrees Capricorn creating an angle of 30 degrees.

Transiting Neptune
Neptune is at 29 degrees Capricorn, so we look for planets from 26 to 2 degrees.

The Sun is at 2 degrees Scorpio creating an aspect of 90 degrees, a square

Midheaven is at 2 degrees Leo creating an aspect of 180 degrees, an opposition.

Transiting Pluto
Pluto is at 5 degrees Sagittarius, so we look for planets from 2 degrees to 8 degrees.

Sun is at 2 degrees Scorpio creating angle of 30 degrees.

Moon is at 3 degrees Aquarius creating an angle of 60 degrees.

Venus is at 4 degrees Sagittarius creating a conjunction.

Midheaven is at 2 degrees Leo creating an angle of 120 degrees, a trine.

Transiting Chiron is at 18 degrees Scorpio, so we look for planets from 15 to 21 degrees.

Mercury is at 21 degrees Scorpio creating a conjunction.

Jupiter is at 17 degrees Taurus creating an aspect of 180 degrees, an opposition.
Saturn is at 19 degrees Libra creating an angle of 30 degrees.

Uranus is at 18 degrees Cancer creating an aspect of 120 degrees, a trine.

Neptune is at 21 degrees Libra creating an angle of 30 degrees.

Having collected the information, we now need to decide what it all means. It might be easy at this point, to have copies of the previous pages containing information about Sophie's 'Planets in Signs' - part of Chapter 7 and the pages on how the planets interact with each other - part of Chapter 8.

On a clean sheet of paper, draw a margin down the left hand side of the page, about a quarter of the width in. In the narrow left-hand column, note down all the transits that create aspects with Sophie's natal chart. (Put a capital 'T' in front of the planet that is transiting, so you can tell the difference!)

Think about the effect the transiting planetary energy will have on the organ or body system indicated by Sophie's natal planets. Note down your thoughts, keeping it really simple, preferably with single keywords until you are more practised.

Transit	Possible Effect
T Sun square Mars	Need to bring balance (☉♎) to adrenals, to muscles affecting knees (♂♑)
T Mercury square Mars	Need to communicate honestly (☿♎) about state of personal energy (♂♑)
T Mars conjunct Pluto	Energy for survival (♂ ♌) directed into transformation & healing (♇ ♌)
T Jupiter trine Mercury	Increase or expansion (♃) of thyroid activity, nerves, thoughts (☿)
T Jupiter quincunx Saturn	Increased (♃) difficulty with stiff joints, frustration, restriction (♄)
T Jupiter Trine Uranus	Increase (♃) in levels of tension (♅), opportunity (♃) for sudden change (♅)
T Jupiter quincunx Neptune	Increased (♃) difficulty with hidden problems or water retention (♆)
T Jupiter quincunx Ascendant	Increased (♃) difficulty how she put herself across to others (Asc)
T Saturn opposition Sun	Inhibition or slowing down (♄) creates tension in life energy affecting the immune system (☉)
T Saturn square Moon	Restriction (♄) in fluid flow (☽) creates a need to take action to release it
T Saturn quincunx Venus	A slowing down (♄) of the hormone system (♀) creates difficulties
T Saturn square Midheaven	Loss of flexibility (♄) creates a need to be seen (MC) to do something dramatic
T Neptune square Sun	Confusion (♆) creates conflicts in her life-energy affecting the immune system (☉)
T Neptune opposition Midheaven	Dissipation of energy (♆) creates tension with a need to be seen (MC) to do something for herself
T Pluto conjunct Venus	Transformation and change (♇) in the way the hormone system works (♀)
T Pluto trine Midheaven	Easy changes (♇) in how she want to appear to others or in her career (MC)
T Chiron conjunct Mercury	A chance to resolve or heal (⚷) her communication ability and settle her nervous system (☿)
T Chiron opposition Jupiter	Tension between the need to heal (⚷) and the love of the good life which pressurises her liver (♃)
T Chiron trine Uranus	A good time to heal (⚷) by creating changes (♅)

Example for Sophie's information:
Figure 38 - Transits Table for Sophie

Looking down the table of information some observations can be made using the information in this book.

1) Pluto stays in one place for a long time due to its slow movement. The transits created by Pluto will have been happening or will be happening for a while - usually about 2 - 3 years. Looking at the two transits, even though Sophie is only 46 years old, one could guess that her hormones are changing and that she might be experiencing some menopausal problems. It would also emphasise any problems with the thyroid or kidneys. The trine to the Midheaven would also suggest that she may need to make some changes in her career.

You could find out how long Pluto has been close to conjunction with Venus, by looking through the ephemeris in the months before September 1998 and in the months after. In January 1997 Pluto first became conjunct Venus. Due to the way Pluto seems to move when viewed from the Earth, it passed Venus again in late April 1997, going retrograde. Pluto passed Venus, going direct again, in November 1997. The core of Sophie's issues reflected by Pluto would have probably started in 1997. However, the data for September 1998, shows Pluto in retrograde again, but this time not becoming exactly conjunct her Venus, before finally moving away. This could hint that she has re-experienced symptoms that she thought she had got rid of or, that she had another chance to deal with them as she had failed to do so earlier.

2) The next slow-moving planet, Neptune is renowned for dissolving what it touches. From a health point of view, for Sophie, it touches the immune system. This would suggest that she feels very tired, run down and has little enthusiasm to do something about how she feels.

3) Saturn slows everything down, but it also ensures things get dealt with properly. Creating four aspects to her natal

chart, it emphasises the slowing down of the hormonal system and the loss of drive and the resulting frustration that occurs. It also suggests that she needs to slow down and reassess her plans and ambitions.

4) Jupiter touches all the areas of other transits, expanding them and making them seem larger, but it also brings an opportunity to get out of the situation. Its contact with Uranus fuels the need to sort the situation out.

5) Mars transits only last a few days. Interestingly here we have Mars conjunct Pluto, giving the needed kick to sort things out.

6) Mercury transits are also only a few days long. Here we have a mental reappraisal of the state of the body and its energy levels.

7) The transit of the Sun, also only effective for a few days at most, that fires the need to act to create balance.

8) Finally, the transits of Chiron should further fuel the desire to heal herself. Dealing with Chiron issues now could lift the pressure of healing crises that could arise when she experiences her Chiron Return. (A 'return' is when a planet transits to the same place as it was in the natal chart.) For Sophie, the Chiron return occurs in 2002.

9) The quincunxes need careful examination, especially the ones created by the slow-moving planets, to see whether any of them are linked to the meridians of Traditional Chinese Medicine.

T Jupiter quincunx Saturn - involves Pisces and Libra
T Jupiter quincunx Neptune - involves Pisces and Libra
T Jupiter quincunx Ascendant - involves Pisces and Libra
T Saturn quincunx Venus - involves Taurus and Sagittarius

None of these match the quincunxes associated with the meridians.

If they did, it would suggest that acupuncture, shiatsu or kinesiology could be needed to stabilise the energy of the body. The type of imbalances created by slow transits can be very debilitating. The symptoms can also seem to be so obscure that orthodox approaches are unable to identify the problem.

If the listing created is dominated by one particular planet, you can focus on that planet's health correspondences to target healing that may be of use.

When you have gathered all your information possible approaches to healing can be taken from the planets identified, both the transiting planet and the natal.

In Sophie's case, we could suggest the following:

Transiting Pluto with its contact with Venus shows an need to transform the way she looks at herself and the way she thinks the world around her works. This can be done effectively with affirmations. To support this and to help with any physical difficulties, a series of aromatherapy sessions or reflexology could be beneficial.

Transiting Neptune's contacts with the Sun may have brought immune system problems like allergies and intolerances to the surface. Simplifying her diet, cutting down on sugar, alcohol and using visualisations to ground her energy would help.

Transiting Chiron could find her looking into herbal healing for her liver problems may lead to a desire to learn more about herbs, organic foods and permaculture. Any knowledge gained under the tutelage of Chiron could potentially be communicated to others.

Transiting Saturn returns to the idea of needing some sort of physical therapy to keep the joints loose and the muscles moving. The Biochemic Tissue Salts would also be indicated here.

Transiting Jupiter re- emphasises the need for good quality food and the reduction of social excesses that pressurise the liver.

Transiting Mars shows the need to act on the problems that are experienced and to take up some gentle exercising.

Transiting Mercury confirms the need to take time out to be quiet and possibly by herself, so that she can relax.

Transiting Sun links with the time of year the transits occurred. Here it is the beginning of autumn and she may instinctively already be noticing the shortening of the days and the daylight available. She could be advised to watch how she reacts to rainy days and if it aggravates how she feels, to invest in some full spectrum lighting for the winter.

Using this technique as a pro-active approach to health

You can use the idea of transits as a guide to the maintenance of health and well-being. The easiest way to do this is to look at a chart, say, every six months. Check out the transits for the coming six months. Pay particular attention to the very slow moving planets. These will highlight underlying trends that you can tackle with Biochemic Tissue Salts, Bach Flower Remedies or therapies linked to the planets. Forewarned is forearmed!

If you know that the individual whose chart you are studying has difficulties with specific organs or body systems, be alert for transits to the planet associated with those areas. This can give you plenty of time to take precautionary measures or to step up any healing or nutrition to help the body deal with those times by following the healing strategies from Chapter 9.

Chapter 12

Further Exploration for the Spiritual Path

When we embark on our spiritual path there are times, when meeting the challenges along the way, that create unique changes in the way the body works.

By applying Worksheet 2 with a different set of planetary rulers, different Biochemic Tissue Salts and Bach Flower Remedies are highlighted to help with well-being.

The set of planetary rulers, called the 'esoteric' rulers used for this worksheet, Worksheet 4 are taken from the work of Alice Bailey and her Guide, Djwhal Khul.

In her book *Esoteric Astrology* she proposed two sets of rulers for two types of people. The orthodox set of rulers she thought related to the 'undeveloped and average man'. The new combination of rulers, she suggested, was for those 'upon the Path'. Alice Bailey went on to explain that there were many ways that various combinations of rulers could reflect different stages of evolution.

Personal experience gained through over thirty years of observation and insight has shown that the frequent effects of starting on the Path are often temporary ill-health and emotional chaos as the energies of the individual start to change.

Vibrational healing can often be the main source of help (tissue salts, essences, etc). Each time the individual's energies shift, a new 'settling-in' time occurs, when again vibrational healing can be very useful.

Sign	Sign	Modern Ruler	Glyph	Esoteric Ruler	Glyph
♈	Aries	Mars	♂	Mercury	☿
♉	Taurus	Venus	♀	Vulcan	Vu
♊	Gemini	Mercury	☿	Venus	♀
♋	Cancer	Moon	☽	Neptune	♆
♌	Leo	Sun	☉	Sun	☉
♍	Virgo	Mercury	☿	Moon	☽
♎	Libra	Venus	♀	Uranus	♅
♏	Scorpio	Pluto	♇	Mars	♂
♐	Sagittarius	Jupiter	♃	Earth	☉
♑	Capricorn	Saturn	♄	Saturn	♄
♒	Aquarius	Uranus	♅	Jupiter	♃
♓	Pisces	Neptune	♆	Pluto	♇

Figure 39 - Esoteric Rulers of the Signs of the Zodiac

By looking at the natal chart, but this time applying Alice Bailey's esoteric set of rulers for the planets, those changes can be integrated more easily.

The two names of planets that are new to this table are Vulcan and the Earth.

Vulcan is taken as the 'heart of the Sun' and sometimes thought of as the potential balance with the Sun, whose presence is felt but never seen. Vulcan always appears within 3 degrees of the Sun. It is left to the intuition of the astrologer as to where exactly that is.

The Earth is always exactly opposite to the Sun in a natal chart.

If we apply this new set of rulers to Worksheet 4, for Sophie we have:

The dominant element and modes for Sophie are Water - 10/Cardinal -14, and Water/Fixed-15, which are related to Cancer and Scorpio.

The lacking combination is Fire - 4/Mutable, which is linked to Sagittarius.

The Biochemic Tissue Salts that these combinations relate to are Calc Fluor (Cancer), Calc Sulph (Scorpio) and Silica (Sagittarius).

These are found in the bones, connective tissue, blood and liver. They all help with skin problems.

The Bach Flower Remedies relating to the combinations are Rock Rose (Cancer), Chicory (Scorpio) and Agrimony (Sagittarius). This happens to be a common association when one is holding onto emotional pain.

These are very different combinations than was found with Worksheet 2 and show Sophie's needs as she embarks on and meets the challenges of her spiritual path. The combinations determined by the esoteric rulers are a useful stand-by as we transform ourselves by spiritual growth.

Figure 40 - Worksheet 4 for Sophie.

Planet	Planet	Sign	Sign	Element	Mode	Esoteric Ruler	Ruler's sign	Element	Mode
☉	Sun	♏	Scorpio	Water	Fixed	Mars	Capricorn	Earth	Card
☽	Moon	♒	Aquarius	Air	Fixed	Jupiter	Taurus	Earth	Fixed
☿	Mercury	♏	Scorpio	Water	Fixed	Mars	Capricorn	Earth	Card
♀	Venus	♐	Sagittarius	Fire	Mut	Earth	Taurus	Earth	Fixed
♂	Mars	♑	Capricorn	Earth	Card	Saturn	Libra	Air	Card
♃	Jupiter	♉	Taurus	Earth	Fixed	Vulcan	Scorpio	Water	Fixed
♄	Saturn	♎	Libra	Air	Card	Uranus	Cancer	Water	Card
♅	Uranus	♋	Cancer	Water	Card	Neptune	Libra	Air	Card
♆	Neptune	♎	Libra	Air	Card	Uranus	Cancer	Water	Card
♇	Pluto	♌	Leo	Fire	Fixed	Sun	Scorpio	Water	Fixed
⚷	Chiron	♑	Capricorn	Earth	Card	Saturn	Libra	Air	Card
As	Asc	♎	Libra	Air	Card	Uranus	Cancer	Water	Card
Mc	MC	♌	Leo	Fire	Fixed	Sun	Scorpio	Water	Fixed
☊	N Node	♒	Aquarius	Air	Fixed	Jupiter	Taurus	Earth	Fixed
☋	S Node	♌	Leo	Fire	Fixed	Sun	Scorpio	Water	Fixed

Element	Total	Mode	Total
Fire	4	Cardinal	14
Earth	8	Fixed	15
Air	8	Mutable	1
Water	10		

Appendix 1 - Sophie's Astrological Chart

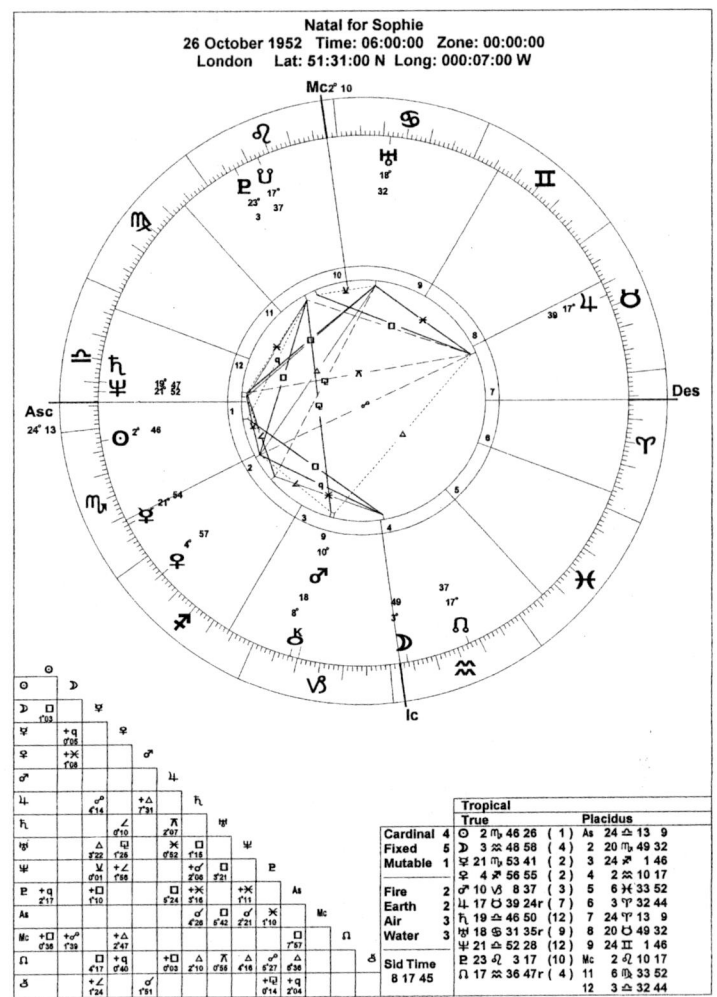

Appendix 2 - Robert's Astrological Chart

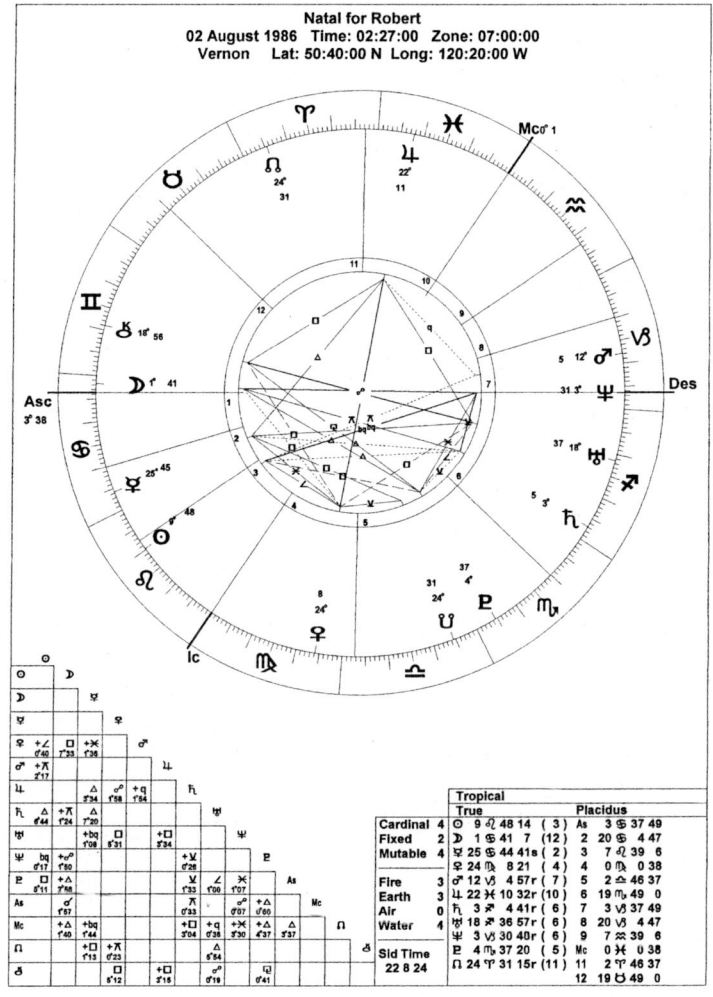

113

Appendix 3

ASTROLOGICAL CORRESPONDENCES

SIGNS – How energy is used & where the energy is most evident

Sign	Body Part	Chakra	Skeleton	Type of Energy
Aries	Head	Crown, Brow	Cranium	Immediate energy, short lasting
Taurus	Neck, throat, mouth, nose, ears	Throat	Cervical	Steady, slow energy, stubborn
Gemini	Lungs, arms, hands, inhalation	Heart	Thoracic	Restless, erratic, unreliable
Cancer	Stomach, membranes	Solar plexus	Thoracic	Strong, sensitive, rhythmical
Leo	Heart	Heart	Thoracic	Sustaining energy
Virgo	Duodenum, small intestine, pancreas, spleen	Solar Plexus	Lumbar	Discriminating, easily influenced by stress
Libra	Kidneys, bladder	S/plexus, Sacral	Sacrum	Needs harmony to function well
Scorpio	Large Intestine, gonads	Sacral	Coccyx	Deep, intense, resistant
Sagittarius	Hips, thighs, exhalation	Base		Fluctuating energy, expansive
Capricorn	Knees, gallbladder	Base		Slow, purposeful, strong
Aquarius	Ankles, uptake of oxygen, circulation	Base		Strong, needs room to
Pisces	Feet, lymph system	base		Easily influenced

PLANETS – Organs

Sun	Heart, eyes, immune system
Moon	Body fluids, lymphatic, menstrual cycle, fertility, eyes
Mercury	Nervous system, mental faculties, thyroid
Venus	Glands, hormones, kidneys, thyroid
Mars	Prana, adrenals, gonads, muscles, inflammation
Jupiter	Liver, left brain
Saturn	Bones, teeth
Uranus	Nervous system, muscle spasms
Neptune	Masks things, weakens, lymphatic system, right brain, pineal
Pluto	Cell transformation, DNA
Chiron	Immune system, thymus gland

Meridians

Aries	Kidney	Scorpio	Bladder
Gemini	Liver	Capricorn	Gall Bladder
Virgo	Large Intestine	Aquarius	Lung
Cancer	Stomach	Sagittarius	Spleen
Taurus	T. Heater	Libra	H. Protector, Cx
Leo	Heart	Pisces	Small Intestine

Appendix 4 Worksheet 1

For:

Planet	Planet	Sign (Glyph)	Sign (Name)	Element	Mode/Action
☉	Sun				
☽	Moon				
☿	Mercury				
♀	Venus				
♂	Mars				
♃	Jupiter				
♄	Saturn				
♅	Uranus				
♆	Neptune				
♇	Pluto				
⚷	Chiron				
As	Ascendant				
Mc	Midheaven				
☊	North Node				
☋	South Node				

Totals:

Element	Element Total	Mode	Mode Total
Fire		Cardinal	
Earth		Fixed	
Air		Mutable	
Water			

Appendix 5 Worksheet 2

For:

Planet	Planet	Sign (Glyph)	Sign (Name)	Element	Mode	Ruler (Planet)	Ruler's Sign	Element	Mode
☉	Sun								
☽	Moon								
☿	Mercury								
♀	Venus								
♂	Mars								
♃	Jupiter								
♄	Saturn								
♅	Uranus								
♆	Neptune								
♇	Pluto								
⚷	Chiron								
As	Ascendant								
Mc	Midheaven								
☊	North Node								
☋	South Node								

Totals:

Element	Element Total	Mode	Mode Total
Fire		Cardinal	
Earth		Fixed	
Air		Mutable	
Water			

Appendix 6 Body Overview Template

For:

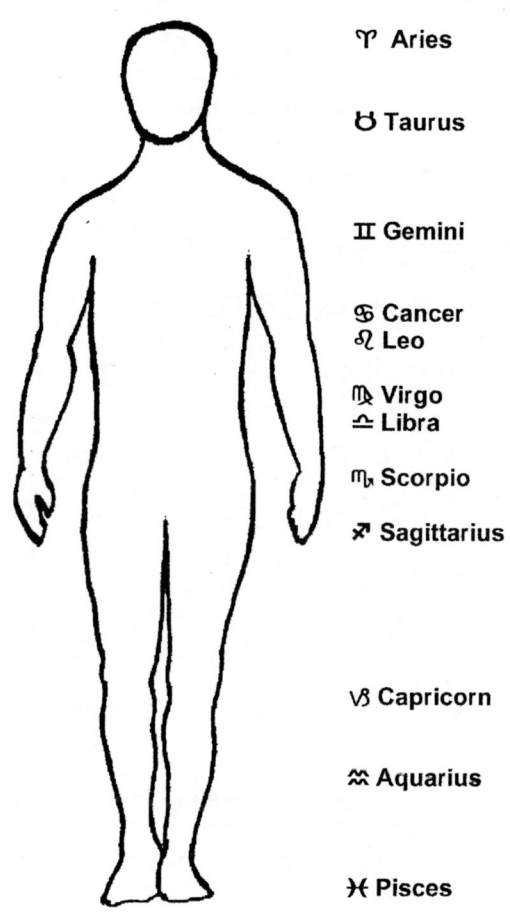

♈ Aries

♉ Taurus

♊ Gemini

♋ Cancer
♌ Leo

♍ Virgo
♎ Libra

♏ Scorpio

♐ Sagittarius

♑ Capricorn

♒ Aquarius

♓ Pisces

Appendix 7

Astrological Correspondences for Green Man Tree Essences

All Green Man Tree Essences are made by the traditional water and sunlight method used by Dr Bach. Full details of each essence can be seen on the Green Man website - www.greenmanessences.com , in the book *'Tree: Essence of Healing'* published by Capall Bann or in the catalogue obtained from Green Man Essences, PO Box 6, Exminster, Exeter Devon, EX6 8YE. A postal sales service from this address operates for the essences themselves.

- ♈ Aries - Holly, Weeping Willow
- ♉ Taurus - Bay, Black Poplar, Gean
- ♊ Gemini - Pittespora, Cedar of Lebanon
- ♋ Cancer - Blackthorn, Italian Alder, Field Maple, Wayfaring Tree
- ♌ Leo - Crack Willow, Medlar
- ♍ Virgo - Hazel, Lucombe Oak, Ash
- ♎ Libra - Glastonbury Thorn, Plane Tree
- ♏ Scorpio - Holm Oak, Bird Cherry, Mulberry
- ♐ Sagittarius - Sweet Chestnut, Tamarisk, Midland Hawthorn
- ♑ Capricorn - Great Sallow, Lawson Cypress, Spindle
- ♒ Aquarius - Tree Lichen, White Willow
- ♓ Pisces - Whitebeam, Red Chestnut, Wych Elm

Planets

- ☉ Sun - Hawthorn, Monkey Puzzle, Manna Ash
- ☽ Moon - Lime, Cherry Plum
- ☿ Mercury - English Elm, Box, Ivy, Mimosa
- ♀ Venus - Silver Birch, Elder, Norway Maple
- ♂ Mars - Viburnum, Osier
- ♃ Jupiter - Beech, Tree of Heaven, Yellow Buckeye
- ♄ Saturn - Lilac, Rowan, Red Oak, Leyland Cypress
- ♅ Uranus - Horse Chestnut, Stags Horn Sumach, Judas Tree
- ♆ Neptune - Strawberry Tree, Scots Pine
- ♇ Pluto - Apple, Laburnum, White Poplar, Monterey Pine
- ⚷ Chiron - Larch, Privet

Elements

Fire - Hornbeam, Plum

Earth - Yew, Catalpa, Gorse

Air - Sycamore, Cherry Laurel

Water - Copper Beech, Tulip Tree, Alder

Modes of Action

Cardinal - Oak, Pear

Fixed - Persian Ironwood, Great Redwood

Mutable - Silver Maple, Magnolia

Worksheet 4 - Esoteric Rulers

Planet	Planet	Sign	Sign	Element	Mode	Esoteric Ruler	Ruler's sign	Element	Mode
☉	Sun								
☽	Moon								
☿	Mercury								
♀	Venus								
♂	Mars								
♃	Jupiter								
♄	Saturn								
♅	Uranus								
♆	Neptune								
♇	Pluto								
⚷	Chiron								
As	Asc								
Mc	MC								
☊	N Node								
☋	S Node								

Element	Total	Mode	Total
Fire		Cardinal	
Earth		Fixed	
Air		Mutable	
Water			

Appendix 8

Bibliography

Baigent M, Campion N, Harvey C, *Mundane Astrology,* Aquarian Press 1984
Barnard, Julian edit, *Collected Writings of Edward Bach,* Ashgrove 1994
Barnard, Julian, *Patterns of Life Force,* Bach Educational Programme 1987
Barnard J & M, *The Healing Herbs of Edward Bach,* Ashgrove 1988
Diamond, John, *Life Energy,* Dodd, Mead, 1985
Ebertin, Reinhold, *The Combination of Stellar Influences,* AFA 1972
Filbey, J, *Natal Charting,* Aquarian 1981
Goodwin, J, *Biochemic Handbook,* Thorsons 1980
Lilly & Lilly, *Tree: Essence of Healing,* Capall Bann 1999
Mann, A.T., *Astrology and The Art of Healing,* Unwin 1989
Pert, Candace, *Molecules of Emotion,* Simon and Schuster 1997
Stein, Zane.B, *A view from Chiron,* CAO Times 1986
Weeks, Nora, *The Discoveries of Edward Bach, Physician,* Daniels 1940

Suggested Reading
Darling, Harry F, *Essentials of Medical Astrology,* AFA 1981, ISBN 0-86690-004-7
Diamond, John, *Your Body Does Not Lie*, Warner ISBN 0446358479
Hay, Louise, *You Can Heal You Life,* Eden Grove, ISBN 1870845013
Jansky, Robert Carl, *Astrology, Nutrition & Health,* Para Research 1977, ISBN 0-914918-08-7
Nauman, Eileen, *Medical Astrology,* Blue Turtle, 1982, ISBN 0-9634662-4

Ridder-Patrick, Jane, *The Handbook of Medical Astrology,* Arkana 1990, ISBN 0-14-019214-X
Sawtell, Vanda, *Astrology and Biochemistry,* Thorsons 1982 ISBN 0-7225-0778-X
Smith, Elaine, *Astrology, The Inner Eye,* Capall Bann 1997 ISBN 186163003-4
Warren-Davis, Dylan, *Astrology and Health*, Hodder & Stoughton, 1998, ISBN 0-33340-70518-3
Wilde, Stuart, *The Trick to Money is Having Some,* Hay House, 1561701688
Williamson, Vivien, *Bach Flower Remedies,* Lorenz, 2001, ISBN 075480626X

Appendix 9

Useful Addresses

Computer Software
Astrocalc
67 Peascroft Road
Hemel Hempstead
Herts
HP3 8ER
England

Tel: +44(0)1442 251809
Fax: +44(0)1422 248902
Email: info@astrocalc.com
Web: www.astrocalc.com

Bach Flower Remedies

Healing Herbs
PO Box 65
Hereford
HR2 0UW
Tel: +44(0)1873 890218
Fax: +44(0)1873 890314
Email: healing-herbs@healing-herbs.co.uk
Web: www.healing-herbs.co.uk

Ainsworths
36 New Cavendish Street
London
W1M 7LH
Tel: 020 7935 5330
Fax: 020 7486 4313
Email: ainshom@msn.com
Web: www.ainsworths.com

Other Flower Essences

Green Man Essences
PO Box 6
Exminster
Exeter, Devon
EX6 8YE
Tel/Fax:+44(0)1392832005
Email: info@greenmanessences.com
Web: www.greenmanessences.com

UK and Europe Essence Producers listing

Web: www.bfvea.com

Chart Providers

Equinox
The Astrology Shop
78 Neal Street
Covent Garden
London WC2H 9PA
Tel: 020 7497 1001
   (various prices from £8)

Mandragora Complementary Studies
PO Box 6
Exminster
Exeter, Devon
EX6 8YE
Tel/Fax: 01392 832005
(£1 per chart or 4x 1st Class postage stamps)

Astrology Courses

Advisory Panel for Astrological
Education
396 Caledonian Road
London, N1 1DN

British Astrological &Psychic Society
PO Box 363
Rochester, Kent
ME1 3DJ
Tel: 0906 4700827
web: www.baps.ws

Mandragora Complementary Studies
 (address as above)

Books
Any good bookshop can order for you

Midheaven Bookshop
396 Caledonian Road
London
N1 1DN

Some of the main Alternative and Complementary
Professional Bodies for therapies mentioned
Registers of Practitioners are available from these addresses.

British Acupuncture Council
63 Jeddo Road
London
W12 9HQ
Tel: 020 8735 0400

Aromatherapy Organisations Council
PO Box 19834
London
SE25 6WF
Tel: 020 8251 7912

British Association for Applied Chiropractic
The Old Post office
Cherry St
Stratton Audley, Oxon
OX6 9BA
Tel: 01869 277111

British Flower and Vibrational Essences Association
8 Willow Glen
Branton
Doncaster
Yorks.
DN3 3JD
Tel: 02092 251 464

British Homeopathic Association
27a Devonshire St
London
W1N 1RJ
Tel: 020 7935 2163

Kinesiology Federation
PO Box 17153
Edinburgh
EH11 3WQ
Tel: 08700 113545

National Institute of Medical Herbalists
56 Longbrook Street
Exeter
EX4 6AH
Tel: 01392 426022

The General Osteopathic Council
176 Tower Bridge Road
London
SE1 3LU
Tel: 020 7357 6655

Association of Reflexologists
27 Old Gloucester St
London
WC1N 3XX
Tel: 0870 5673320

Shiatsu Society
Eastlands Court
St Peters Road
Rugby
CV21 3QP
Tel: 01788 555051

FREE DETAILED CATALOGUE

Capall Bann is owned and run by people actively involved in many of the areas in which we publish. A detailed illustrated catalogue is available on request, SAE or International Postal Coupon appreciated. **Titles can be ordered direct from Capall Bann, post free in the UK** (cheque or PO with order) or from good bookshops and specialist outlets.

Do contact us for details on the latest releases at: **Capall Bann Publishing, Freshfields, Chieveley, Berks, RG20 8TF.** Titles include:

A Breath Behind Time, Terri Hector
Angels and Goddesses - Celtic Christianity & Paganism, M. Howard
Arthur - The Legend Unveiled, C Johnson & E Lung
Astrology The Inner Eye - A Guide in Everyday Language, E Smith
Auguries and Omens - The Magical Lore of Birds, Yvonne Aburrow
Asyniur - Womens Mysteries in the Northern Tradition, S McGrath
Beginnings - Geomancy, Builder's Rites & Electional Astrology in the European Tradition, Nigel Pennick
Between Earth and Sky, Julia Day
Book of the Veil , Peter Paddon
Caer Sidhe - Celtic Astrology and Astronomy, Vol 1, Michael Bayley
Caer Sidhe - Celtic Astrology and Astronomy, Vol 2 M Bayley
Call of the Horned Piper, Nigel Jackson
Cat's Company, Ann Walker
Celtic Faery Shamanism, Catrin James
Celtic Faery Shamanism - The Wisdom of the Otherworld, Catrin James
Celtic Lore & Druidic Ritual, Rhiannon Ryall
Celtic Sacrifice - Pre Christian Ritual & Religion, Marion Pearce
Celtic Saints and the Glastonbury Zodiac, Mary Caine
Circle and the Square, Jack Gale
Compleat Vampyre - The Vampyre Shaman, Nigel Jackson
Creating Form From the Mist - The Wisdom of Women in Celtic Myth and Culture, Lynne Sinclair-Wood
Crystal Clear - A Guide to Quartz Crystal, Jennifer Dent
Crystal Doorways, Simon & Sue Lilly
Crossing the Borderlines - Guising, Masking & Ritual Animal Disguise in the European Tradition, Nigel Pennick
Dragons of the West, Nigel Pennick
Earth Dance - A Year of Pagan Rituals, Jan Brodie
Earth Harmony - Places of Power, Holiness & Healing, Nigel Pennick
Earth Magic, Margaret McArthur

Eildon Tree (The) Romany Language & Lore, Michael Hoadley
Enchanted Forest - The Magical Lore of Trees, Yvonne Aburrow
Eternal Priestess, Sage Weston
Eternally Yours Faithfully, Roy Radford & Evelyn Gregory
Everything You Always Wanted To Know About Your Body, But So Far Nobody's Been Able To Tell You, Chris Thomas & D Baker
Face of the Deep - Healing Body & Soul, Penny Allen
Fairies in the Irish Tradition, Molly Gowen
Familiars - Animal Powers of Britain, Anna Franklin
Fool's First Steps, (The) Chris Thomas
Forest Paths - Tree Divination, Brian Harrison, Ill. S. Rouse
From Past to Future Life, Dr Roger Webber
Gardening For Wildlife Ron Wilson
God Year, The, Nigel Pennick & Helen Field
Goddess on the Cross, Dr George Young
Goddess Year, The, Nigel Pennick & Helen Field
Goddesses, Guardians & Groves, Jack Gale
Handbook For Pagan Healers, Liz Joan
Handbook of Fairies, Ronan Coghlan
Healing Book, The, Chris Thomas and Diane Baker
Healing Homes, Jennifer Dent
Healing Journeys, Paul Williamson
Healing Stones, Sue Philips
Herb Craft - Shamanic & Ritual Use of Herbs, Lavender & Franklin
Hidden Heritage - Exploring Ancient Essex, Terry Johnson
Hub of the Wheel, Skytoucher
In Search of Herne the Hunter, Eric Fitch
Inner Celtia, Alan Richardson & David Annwn
Inner Mysteries of the Goths, Nigel Pennick
Inner Space Workbook - Develop Thru Tarot, C Summers & J Vayne
Intuitive Journey, Ann Walker Isis - African Queen, Akkadia Ford
Journey Home, The, Chris Thomas
Kecks, Keddles & Kesh - Celtic Lang & The Cog Almanac, Bayley
Language of the Psycards, Berenice
Legend of Robin Hood, The, Richard Rutherford-Moore
Lid Off the Cauldron, Patricia Crowther
Light From the Shadows - Modern Traditional Witchcraft, Gwyn
Living Tarot, Ann Walker
Lore of the Sacred Horse, Marion Davies
Lost Lands & Sunken Cities (2nd ed.), Nigel Pennick
Magic of Herbs - A Complete Home Herbal, Rhiannon Ryall
Magical Guardians - Exploring the Spirit and Nature of Trees, Philip Heselton
Magical History of the Horse, Janet Farrar & Virginia Russell
Magical Lore of Animals, Yvonne Aburrow
Magical Lore of Cats, Marion Davies
Magical Lore of Herbs, Marion Davies

Magick Without Peers, Ariadne Rainbird & David Rankine
Masks of Misrule - Horned God & His Cult in Europe, Nigel Jackson
Medicine For The Coming Age, Lisa Bund MD
Medium Rare - Reminiscences of a Clairvoyant, Muriel Renard
Menopausal Woman on the Run, Jaki da Costa
Mind Massage - 60 Creative Visualisations, Marlene Maundrill
Mirrors of Magic - Evoking the Spirit of the Dewponds, P Heselton
Moon Mysteries, Jan Brodie
Mysteries of the Runes, Michael Howard
Mystic Life of Animals, Ann Walker
New Celtic Oracle The, Nigel Pennick & Nigel Jackson
Oracle of Geomancy, Nigel Pennick
Pagan Feasts - Seasonal Food for the 8 Festivals, Franklin & Phillips
Patchwork of Magic - Living in a Pagan World, Julia Day
Pathworking - A Practical Book of Guided Meditations, Pete Jennings
Personal Power, Anna Franklin
Pickingill Papers - The Origins of Gardnerian Wicca, Bill Liddell
Pillars of Tubal Cain, Nigel Jackson
Places of Pilgrimage and Healing, Adrian Cooper
Practical Divining, Richard Foord
Practical Meditation, Steve Hounsome
Practical Spirituality, Steve Hounsome
Psychic Self Defence - Real Solutions, Jan Brodie
Real Fairies, David Tame
Reality - How It Works & Why It Mostly Doesn't, Rik Dent
Romany Tapestry, Michael Houghton
Runic Astrology, Nigel Pennick
Sacred Animals, Gordon MacLellan
Sacred Celtic Animals, Marion Davies, Ill. Simon Rouse
Sacred Dorset - On the Path of the Dragon, Peter Knight
Sacred Grove - The Mysteries of the Forest, Yvonne Aburrow
Sacred Geometry, Nigel Pennick
Sacred Nature, Ancient Wisdom & Modern Meanings, A Cooper
Sacred Ring - Pagan Origins of British Folk Festivals, M. Howard
Season of Sorcery - On Becoming a Wisewoman, Poppy Palin
Seasonal Magic - Diary of a Village Witch, Paddy Slade
Secret Places of the Goddess, Philip Heselton
Secret Signs & Sigils, Nigel Pennick
Self Enlightenment, Mayan O'Brien
Spirits of the Air, Jaq D Hawkins
Spirits of the Earth, Jaq D Hawkins
Spirits of the Earth, Jaq D Hawkins
Stony Gaze, Investigating Celtic Heads John Billingsley
Stumbling Through the Undergrowth, Mark Kirwan-Heyhoe
Subterranean Kingdom, The, revised 2nd ed, Nigel Pennick
Symbols of Ancient Gods, Rhiannon Ryall

Talking to the Earth, Gordon MacLellan
Taming the Wolf - Full Moon Meditations, Steve Hounsome
Teachings of the Wisewomen, Rhiannon Ryall
The Other Kingdoms Speak, Helena Hawley
Tree: Essence of Healing, Simon & Sue Lilly
Tree: Essence, Spirit & Teacher, Simon & Sue Lilly
Through the Veil, Peter Paddon
Torch and the Spear, Patrick Regan
Understanding Chaos Magic, Jaq D Hawkins
Vortex - The End of History, Mary Russell
Warp and Weft - In Search of the I-Ching, William de Fancourt
Warriors at the Edge of Time, Jan Fry
Water Witches, Tony Steele
Way of the Magus, Michael Howard
Weaving a Web of Magic, Rhiannon Ryall
West Country Wicca, Rhiannon Ryall
Wildwitch - The Craft of the Natural Psychic, Poppy Palin
Wildwood King, Philip Kane
Witches of Oz, Matthew & Julia Philips
Wondrous Land - The Faery Faith of Ireland by Dr Kay Mullin
Working With the Merlin, Geoff Hughes
Your Talking Pet, Ann Walker

FREE detailed catalogue and FREE 'Inspiration' magazine
Contact: Capall Bann Publishing, Freshfields, Chieveley, Berks, RG20 8TF